Contents

D0240832

part of Williams Lea Tag

A Practical Guide to Living in the United Kingdom

Jenny Wales

part of Williams Lea Tag

Published by TSO (The Stationery Office), part of Williams Lea Tag,
and available from:

Online
www.tsoshop.co.uk

Mail, Telephone, Fax & E-mail
TSO
PO Box 29, Norwich, NR3 1GN
Telephone orders/General enquiries: 0333 202 5070
Fax orders: 0333 202 5080
E-mail: customer.services@tso.co.uk
Textphone 0333 202 5077

TSO@Blackwell and other Accredited Agents

The information contained in this publication is believed to be correct at
the time of manufacture. Whilst care has been taken to ensure that the
information is accurate, the publisher can accept no responsibility for any
errors or omissions or for changes to the details given.

ISBN 978 0117082557

First edition, third impression 2017

Printed in the United Kingdom

Acknowledgements

TSO gratefully acknowledges the contributions of the following reviewers:

Damian Brooks
David Kerr

Michael Mitchell
Lorraine Wilson

Photographic credits

Page 7 – *Michael Blann/Photodisc/Thinkstock*

Page 8 – *Stockbyte/Thinkstock*

Page 14 – *GarethPriceGFX/iStock/Thinkstock*

Page 17 – *Oversnap/iStock/Thinkstock*

Page 24 – *Darrensp/iStock/Thinkstock*

Page 28 – *Bravegunner/iStock/Thinkstock*

Page 32 – *Rostislav_Sedlacek/iStock/Thinkstock*

Page 34 – *AmmentorpDK/iStock/Thinkstock*

Page 37 – *Monkeybusinessimages/iStock/Thinkstock*

Page 43 – *Monkeybusinessimages/iStock/Thinkstock*

Page 47 – *JoKP/iStock/Thinkstock*

Page 49 – *David Henderson/iStock/Thinkstock*

Page 53 – *Sinemaslow/iStock/Thinkstock*

Page 56 – *Tommaso Tagliaferri/Stockbyte/Thinkstock*

Page 58 – UK currency coins *Claudiodivizia/iStock/Thinkstock*

Page 58 – Close-up of various UK pound notes *Stockbyte/Thinkstock*

Page 61 – *Klaptoman/iStock/Thinkstock*

Page 63 – *JackF/iStock/Thinkstock*

Page 68 – *Fazon1/iStock/Thinkstock*

Page 69 – *Scyther5/iStock/Thinkstock*

Page 74 – *Jupiterimages/Creatas/Thinkstock*

Page 77 – *Habari1/iStock/Thinkstock*

Page 80 – *Peter Clark/iStock/Thinkstock*

Page 89 – *Monkeybusinessimages/iStock/Thinkstock*

Page 91 – *Mtreasure/iStock/Thinkstock*

Page 97 – *Digital Vision/Thinkstock*

Page 103 – *Monkeybusinessimages/iStock/Thinkstock*

Page 104 – *Ammentorp Photography/iStock/Thinkstock*

Page 106 – *Brand X Pictures/iStock/Thinkstock*

Page 111 – *Alzram18/iStock/Thinkstock*

Page 117 – *Photos.com/Thinkstock*

Page 119 – *stocksnapper/iStock/Thinkstock*

Page 122 – *Ashley Pickering/iStock/Thinkstock*

Page 128 – *ArminStautBerlin/iStock/Thinkstock*

Page 132 – *Ingram Publishing/Thinkstock*

Page 134 – *Stockbyte/Thinkstock*

Page 137 – Tower Bridge in London *TomasSereda/iStock/Thinkstock*

Page 137 – Bridge, Chatsworth House, Derbyshire *Hemera Technologies/AbleStock.com/Thinkstock*

Page 138 – Brecon Beacons national park *Uppy61/iStock/Thinkstock*

Page 138 – Loch Ness *Jiangli/iStock/Thinkstock*

Page 138 – Mourne Mountains *RogerBradley/iStock/Thinkstock*

Page 140 – *Georgeblomfield/iStock/Thinkstock*

Page 142 – *Andrew J Shearer/iStock/Thinkstock*

Page 143 – *Sarradet/iStock/Thinkstock*

Page 145 – *Zefart/iStock/Thinkstock*

Page 149 – *Monkeybusinessimages/Monkey Business/Thinkstock*

Page 152 – *RyanDeanMorrison/iStock/Thinkstock*

Page 154 – *Nick White/Digital Vision/Thinkstock*

Page 156 – *Fuse/Thinkstock*

Page 158 – *Fuse/Thinkstock*

Page 160 – *John Howard/Digital Vision/Thinkstock*

Page 161 – *Nyul/iStock/Thinkstock*

Introduction

Welcome to the **Practical Guide to Living in the UK**. This book will help you to understand the legal requirements for coming to the UK and provide you with a wide range of interesting information about how people live here.

The book has been written so that you can easily find information on the different aspects of living in the UK. It includes web links that help you to find out more about the topics described, as well as action boxes full of activities for you to try out. The first chapter examines the ways in which the law affects you. It explains the rules about visas and immigration and describes how laws are made. The second chapter explores working life in the UK. It gives a range of guidance on finding a job and goes on to describe your rights and responsibilities when you are at work. There is also a section on the various ways you can set up your own business.

The third chapter deals with everyday life. It covers topics such as the English language and its origins, the currency that is used in the UK, and information on bank accounts and borrowing money. It also provides advice on buying or renting houses or flats, and the legal responsibilities involved.

Chapter 4 covers family life and gives you an idea of the kind of health and education services you are likely to encounter. You will also learn more about marriage laws, children's rights and childcare.

Understanding community life will help you to make friends with people and get involved with local activities. Chapter 5 contains a wealth of information on volunteering, as well as ways to find out more about the UK's museums, festivals and arts scene.

The final chapter provides essential background on the geography of the UK and looks at the customs and traditions you may experience if you travel to different parts of the country. You'll learn more about visiting places of interest, as well as how to get around using public transport.

Living in a new country can be often be a confusing experience - we hope that this book will help you to settle in quickly and enjoy your new life.

Chapter 1

How the law affects you

In this chapter you will learn about:

- Visas and immigration
- National government
- Laws and the legal system

Before you arrive

Who needs a visa?

If you are a citizen of the European Economic Area (EEA) or Switzerland, in most cases you will not need a visa. There are some restrictions on Croatian nationals who wish to work in the UK.

If you live outside this area, you should check the rules before you apply. You can find help and guidance on the **gov.uk** website, where you will also find useful tools to help you decide what visa you will need. The gov.uk website is designed to help people – and businesses – access important government services and information.

? Web help

Do I need a visa to work or study in the UK?
www.gov.uk/check-uk-visa

Short-stay visas

People wishing to work or study in the UK for up to six months can apply for visas in the following short-stay categories:

- **Business Visitor** – This category includes three different types of visa: business visitor; academic visitor; and doctors and dentists.
- **Prospective Entrepreneur** – This visa is for people who are intending to secure funding to take over, join or run a UK-based business. It is also suitable for people wanting to finance new businesses.
- **Permitted Paid Engagement** – This is for people who want to work for a period of up to one month in specific paid jobs.

- **Sports Visitor** – This is for people who are competing in (or working as support staff at) a specific sporting event.
- **Entertainer Visitor** – This is for entertainers who are expecting to perform in the UK for up to six months.
- **Student Visitor** – This is for students on short courses and programmes of study.

There are also categories of visa for tourists and people visiting family in the UK. You should be aware that each visa has different rules around what you can and can't do with it and the length of time for which it is valid. For more information, check the **gov.uk** website.

[?] Web help

Find out about short-stay visas:

www.gov.uk/browse/visas-immigration/short-stay-visas

Visa tiers

If you would like to work or study in the UK for more than six months, other types of visa are available. The UK uses what is known as a points-based system to decide whether you have a right to one of these visas. There are four tiers in use at the moment, with different categories of visa within each tier:

Tier 1   Highly skilled people, such as scientists and entrepreneurs

Tier 2   Skilled workers with a job offer, such as teachers and nurses

[**Tier 3**   Closed]

Tier 4   Students

Tier 5   Temporary workers with a job offer, such as domestic workers in private homes, representatives of a business, and participants in the youth mobility scheme.

The points are calculated by looking at your qualifications, current work, whether you have been offered a job in the UK and whether you have a sponsor.

To help you work out whether you have enough points for your chosen tier, there is a useful tool on the Home Office website.

 **Web help**

How many points do I have?

https://www.points.homeoffice.gov.uk/gui-migrant-jsf/
SelfAssessment/SelfAssessment.faces

Joining family in the UK

If you are planning to move to be with family living in the UK and you're from outside the European Economic Area or Switzerland, you will need to apply for a 'Family of a Settled Person' visa. If your visit is for less than six months, you don't need to apply for this visa, but you may need a Family Visit visa – check on **gov.uk** for more information.

Sponsorship

Most people applying for a UK work visa need a sponsor.

- **Tier 1 applicants** – This requirement does not apply to you unless you are applying for an Exceptional Talent visa.
- **Tiers 2 and 4 applicants** – You must have a sponsor.
- **Tier 5 applicants** – You must have a sponsor unless you are on the youth mobility scheme.[1]

Sponsors must have a licence. They need to apply online and then send their payment and supporting documents by post. Your sponsor must monitor you in your workplace or as a student while you are in the UK. Their responsibilities vary according to your visa tier.

---

1   If you're applying for a visa in the youth mobility category and you're from Hong Kong, the Republic of Korea or Taiwan, you will need sponsorship.

> **? Web help**
>
> **Your sponsor's responsibilities**
>
> www.gov.uk/uk-visa-sponsorship-employers

Applying for a visa

You can apply for a visa online if you plan to visit, work, study or join a family member or partner already in the UK.

What does a visa cost?

The cost of a visa varies – it depends on the type of visa and where you are when you make your application. People applying for different tiers and different categories pay different fees.

> **? Web help**
>
> **Applying for a visa**
>
> https://www.gov.uk/apply-uk-visa
>
> **What will my visa cost?**
>
> https://www.gov.uk/visa-fees

How long does a visa last?

The length of your visa will depend on:

- the tier of the visa
- the category of visa within the tier.

You can also apply to extend your visa should it expire, although there are some limits. You can find out more from the **gov.uk** website.

Checklist for people with jobs

The range of documents you need to bring with you depends on your visa tier. You must check carefully to make sure you have all those that are needed.

> ### ? Web help
>
> **Which documents do I need to bring?**
>
> **www.gov.uk/uk-border-control/before-you-leave-for-the-uk**

Settling in the UK permanently

Permanent settlement in the UK is known as 'permanent leave to remain'.

You may be able to apply for naturalisation as a British citizen if:

- you are over 18 and have been living in the UK for the last five years.
- you are over 18 and are married to (or are the civil partner of) a British citizen and have been living here for the last three years.
- you or your husband, wife or civil partner is working for the British government outside the UK.

Everyone who applies must have passed the Life in the UK test and hold a language qualification.

You will also need to meet certain other requirements and conditions.

> ### ? Web help
>
> **What is the Life in the UK test?**
>
> **www.gov.uk/life-in-the-uk-test**
>
> **What are the requirements for permanent settlement?**
>
> You can apply here for permanent settlement:
> **https://www.gov.uk/settle-in-the-uk**

Remember that the rules on visas and immigration change from time to time as new laws are passed. To keep up to date with the latest information from UK Visas and Immigration, you can sign up to the email alerts service on **gov.uk.**

National government

Laws in the UK, including the ones about visas and immigration, are passed by Parliament.

Parliament is made up of the House of Commons and the House of Lords – both are found in the building shown in the picture. The famous clock tower you can see is now called the Elizabeth Tower (named after the Queen) but it is still usually known as Big Ben. (Big Ben is the name of the largest bell inside the tower.) You may have heard the sound of the clock chiming over the radio on the BBC news.

The House of Commons is fully elected and the House of Lords is made up of people who have been selected by the parliamentary parties and those who have inherited the right.

The Houses of Parliament

Elections

Elections for the national government take place every five years. These are known as General Elections.

In the UK, almost all citizens over the age of 18 can vote in elections. At a General Election, voters elect a Member of Parliament (MP) to represent them in the House of Commons. Most citizens can stand for election too.

If you become a citizen of the UK, you must complete forms to be included in the electoral register. These will be posted to you annually so the register is kept up to date. Once on the register, you will be sent a card at election time to tell you where to vote. The location is known as a polling station and it might be a school or community hall. Your vote is always secret.

UK citizens can also vote for candidates for the European Parliament, regional government (such as the Welsh Assembly) and local government.

The area that an MP represents is known as a constituency and people living in the constituency are called constituents. When sitting in the House of Commons, MPs represent all their constituents, not just those who voted for them. You can contact your MP by email, letter or at their office in the constituency. They have special times to meet their constituents. You find out about these meetings on your MP's website.

Political parties

Most candidates in General Elections represent a political party. The parties with the most representation in Parliament are currently the Conservative Party, the Labour Party and the Liberal Democrats. There are also parties representing Scottish, Welsh and Northern Irish interests.

MPs do not need to belong to a political party – they can be 'independent'. This type of MP usually represents an issue that is important to their constituency.

As an individual, you can join a political party if you want to support its work.

┌───┐

[!] **Action**

Find out more about the political parties of the UK, especially the ones that are active in the area where you live – or are expecting to live – in the UK.

└───┘

The government

The political party with the most MPs in the House of Commons forms the government. If no party has an overall majority (more than half of the elected MPs), parties may need to join together to form a coalition government.

The leader of the party which forms the government becomes the Prime Minister and moves into 10 Downing Street, which is not far from the Houses of Parliament.

The Prime Minister appoints the cabinet. This is the inner group of Ministers who are responsible for government policy. The Chancellor of the Exchequer runs the country's finances from the Treasury. The Home Secretary looks after matters that are important within the UK (such as the police, passports and the control of illegal drugs). The Foreign Secretary is in charge of foreign affairs (which include promoting UK interests overseas and providing support for British nationals working in foreign countries). There are also Secretaries of State, who are in charge of all the other areas, such as business and education.

The Opposition is made up of the MPs belonging to the political parties who did not win in the General Election. The leader of the biggest party appoints the 'shadow cabinet' to challenge the government.

Number 10 Downing Street, home of the British Prime Minister

 **Web help**

What does the Prime Minister do?

Find out about the work of the Prime Minister:
https://www.gov.uk/government/organisations/prime-ministers-office-10-downing-street

---

The work of Parliament

The main work of Parliament is to look carefully at laws that are being proposed and to pass them once they have been agreed. Each year the Queen opens Parliament and in her speech she sets out the laws that the government wants to pass. Until they have been accepted by both the House of Commons and the House of Lords, these draft laws are called Bills. Each Bill is carefully drafted to avoid confusion when it becomes law.

Each Bill is debated in the House of Commons first. The opposing parties will discuss each point and make changes according to the views of the MPs.

Once it has been debated in the House of Commons, the Bill goes to the House of Lords, where it is debated again and amended again if necessary.

Pressure groups and organisations with specific interests may try to influence Parliament's decisions on particular topics, but members of the Houses of Commons and Lords make the final decision.

Eventually, when everything is complete, the Bill turns into a law and the Queen gives it the Royal Assent.

Once a law is in force, the civil service makes sure that laws are carried out. The civil service is the administrative department of the government. It is not political and must be impartial. Parliament makes the law in the UK but judges in the courts interpret it. The government cannot interfere with the courts.

The monarchy

The UK has a constitutional monarchy in which the Queen is the head of the state. As part of her duties, she gives advice to the government but does not make political decisions. The government is elected by the people, but after an election, the new Prime Minister will go to see the Queen to be sworn in.

Queen Elizabeth II came to the throne on her father's death in 1952. Prince Charles (the Prince of Wales) is her oldest son and is the heir to the throne.

The monarch must sign off every law that's passed before it is finalised.

> **! Action**
>
> **Find out the name of your MP. Which party do they represent?**
>
> **What is the name of the constituency where you live?**
>
> **Watch the news on television or read a newspaper to find out what is going on in Parliament.**

Laws and the legal system

People who live in the UK have both **rights and responsibilities** which are set out in law. Everyone has the right to equal treatment - whoever they are and wherever they come from.

Your rights

The Human Rights Act

These rights are set out in British law in the Human Rights Act 1998 and apply to everyone in the UK. Public bodies such as the police, schools and hospitals have to work in a way that follows the Human Rights Act.

> **? Web help**
>
> There is more information on the Human Rights Act on the UK legislation website:
>
> **www.legislation.gov.uk/ukpga/1998/42/contents**

Equal opportunities

Laws ensure that people are not treated unfairly because of their sex, race, disability, sexuality, religion, age or class. These laws apply in all areas of life, including your place of work.

If you face problems with discrimination, you can get more information from the Citizens Advice Bureau (CAB). The CAB can give you advice over the phone or you can visit one of their offices – they can be found in many towns in England and Wales. They also have a useful website.

? Web help

Organisations which offer help

- England and Wales: Equality and Human Rights Commission (**www.equalityhumanrights.com**)
- Scotland: Equality and Human Rights Commission in Scotland (**www.equalityhumanrights.com/scotland/the-commission-in-scotland**) and Scottish Human Rights Commission (**www.scottishhumanrights.com**)
- Northern Ireland: Equality Commission for Northern Ireland (**www.equalityni.org**) and Northern Ireland Human Rights Commission (**www.nihrc.org**)
- Citizens Advice Bureau (**www.citizensadvice.org.uk**)

Your responsibilities

Your responsibility is to obey the law.

There are two types of law:

- criminal law
- civil law.

If you break a criminal law, the police will be involved and you may need to attend one of the criminal courts.

Civil law is used to resolve disputes between people and the civil courts are used to decide who is right and who is wrong.

Criminal law

Laws are passed by Parliament to protect people. If you break a criminal law, you will usually be dealt with by the courts system. Crimes such as murder, theft and assault are criminal offences. There are many more, including those in the diagram. If you commit any of these offences – and many others – you might find yourself in court.

Carry a weapon

Commit racially motivated crime

Sell tobacco to anyone under the age of 18

Behave in an anti-social way

Smoke in enclosed public places

Abuse or harass people because of their religion or ethnic origin

Sell alcohol to anyone who is under 18

Sell and buy drugs

Drink alcohol in alcohol-free zones

Examples of crimes under UK law. Anyone found breaking the law in the UK will be dealt with by the police and the courts system

? **Web help**

Criminal law
You can find details of all UK law here: **www.legislation.gov.uk**

Civil law

Disputes between people are resolved by civil law.

Examples of disputes resolved by civil law

! Action

Have a look at your local newspaper to find out about people who have been found guilty of an offence. What penalty did they receive?

You have responsibilities in your different roles in life:

- Responsibilities at work are in **Chapter 2**
- Responsibilities in everyday life are in **Chapter 3**
- Responsibilities to your family are in **Chapter 4**.

Law enforcement

The police

Protect life
and property

Prevent and
detect crime

Prevent
disturbances - also
known as keeping
the peace

The role of the police in the UK

The police force protects the public and solves crimes. Police officers are independent of government and must obey the law. Their powers are also defined in codes of practice.

When dealing with the public the police must not:

- discriminate against you because of your race, religion, belief, sexual orientation, age or disability
- be abusive (for example, by insulting you or being violent)
- make false statements (this means telling lies – saying they saw you do something when that was not true, for example).

If the police abuse their authority by breaking the law or their code of practice, they can be disciplined or prosecuted.

Police stops

The police have powers that enable them to either stop you or stop and search you.

If they stop you, they might ask why you are in the area, what you are doing, where you are going and what you are carrying.

If they stop and search you, they will search your clothes, bags and anything else you might be carrying.

They must not stop you because of your nationality, faith, ethnicity, language or criminal record. This would be discrimination. Police officers must have a good reason to stop you – for example, if they believe that you are carrying stolen property or a weapon.

Sometimes officers are able to stop and search anyone in an area if they suspect that a serious crime has taken place or may take place in the future.

If the police stop you:

- You don't have to give your personal details (name, age, address, etc.) unless the police officer is reporting you for an offence.

- The officers should provide you with their names, their station and the reason why you are being stopped and searched. They should also show you their warrant card and explain to you what your rights are in this situation.

If you are in a vehicle:

- The police can stop you at any time and ask to see your driving licence and insurance.

- They may also ask you where you are going and why you are going there. It does not become a stop and search unless and until you are asked to leave your vehicle so the officers can search it.

Searching and entering buildings

Police officers don't have the right to enter and search any building unless something serious has happened. They must have a document (called a warrant) which gives them legal permission.

Arrest

The police may ask you to go to a police station to answer more questions. If you go to a police station voluntarily (which means you are willing to go), you can leave when you want to, unless the police arrest you.

If you are rude, violent or decide to mislead the police then you might be arrested.

If you are arrested:

- You will be told why you have been arrested and what crime the police suspect you have committed.

- You will be taken to a police station.

- You will be 'held in custody' at the police station, which means you must stay there for a while. Usually, unless the police charge you with a crime within 24 hours they must allow you to leave.

If English is not your first language, the police should be able to help by providing an interpreter.

Young people

A young person under the age of 18 can only be interviewed if their parent or an 'appropriate adult' is present (this could be a social worker, an adult friend or a teacher).

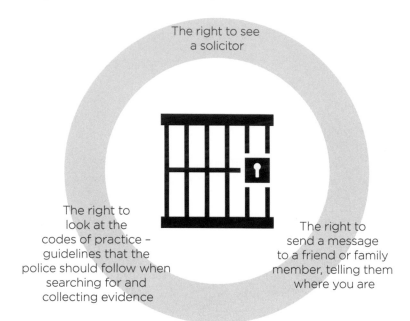

The right to see a solicitor

The right to look at the codes of practice – guidelines that the police should follow when searching for and collecting evidence

The right to send a message to a friend or family member, telling them where you are

Your rights if you are arrested

You will be 'cautioned' before you are questioned.

The caution

The following words are normally spoken to someone who is being arrested:

'You do not have to say anything, but it may harm your defence if you do not mention, when questioned, something which you later rely on in court. Anything you do say may be given in evidence.'

This means that if you do not tell the whole truth when you are interviewed by the police, it may count against you if you appear in court. They will record anything you do say to them and this may be used in court.

The duty solicitor

If you are arrested or go to a police station voluntarily, you are entitled to legal advice in private. This can be with a solicitor that you choose or the duty solicitor. This first meeting does not cost you anything.

You have the right not to answer questions, except to give your name and address, until you have spoken to a solicitor.

Complaints

If you feel that the police have treated you badly, you can complain to the Chief Constable of the area. You can also complain to the Independent Police Complaints Commission (IPCC) in England and Wales. They will usually refer you back to the police force you complained about as they only deal with very serious complaints. If you are still unhappy you can appeal, and this will be dealt with by the IPCC.

Complaints can help the police to improve the way they do things so that they provide a better service in the future.

? Web help

Making a complaint

More information about the IPCC can be found at **www.ipcc.gov.uk**

You can also seek advice from the Citizens Advice Bureau at **www.citizensadvice.org.uk**

In Scotland you can find out more at **www.pcc-scotland.org**

In Northern Ireland you can find out more at **www.policeombudsman.org**

> **[!] Action**
>
> **Find out where your nearest police station is.**
>
> **What phone number do you use in an emergency?**
>
> **What phone number do you use to contact the police if it is not an emergency?**

Criminal courts

If you commit a crime, the type of court that deals with your case will depend on the seriousness of the crime.

Courts for minor offences

Most minor criminal cases in England, Wales and Northern Ireland are dealt with in a Magistrates' Court. In Scotland they are heard in a Justice of the Peace Court.

The Supreme Court, London

Magistrates (who are also known as justices of the peace (JPs)) are members of the local community who usually work unpaid. They do not need legal qualifications but receive special training. Magistrates are supported by a legal adviser, who is known as the court clerk or the clerk to the justices. Magistrates decide whether you are guilty of the offence of which you are accused and if they find that you are then they give the proper penalty.

Courts for more serious offences
The Crown Court is used in England, Wales and Northern Ireland for serious offences. A judge and a jury hear the case and make the decisions. In Scotland, more serious cases are heard in a Sheriff Court with either a sheriff or a sheriff with a jury. The most serious cases – such as murder – are heard at a High Court with a judge and jury.

A jury is made up of members of the public chosen at random from the local electoral register. In England, Wales and Northern Ireland a jury has 12 members, and in Scotland a jury has 15 members. Everyone who is called to do jury service must do it unless they have a very good reason – such as ill health. The jury decides on the verdict. If the verdict is guilty the judge decides on the penalty.

Youth Court
An offender between the ages of 10 and 17 is dealt with in a Youth Court. The magistrates are specially trained to deal with young people. The most serious cases will go to a Crown Court. The parents or carers are expected to attend the hearing, which is private and names and photographs cannot be reported in the media. The Youth Justice Board oversees the youth justice system in England and Wales.

In Scotland the system is a little different. Children who commit offences are dealt with by the Children's Hearings System. Children's reporters are at the heart of the system and are based in local communities. Children and young people are referred to the reporter by the police, social work, schools and the healthcare system because some aspect of their life is giving cause for concern.

If the reporter thinks compulsory measures of intervention are needed, a children's hearing will be held. There will be three panel members who are trained volunteers from the local community.

The hearing considers the child's circumstances and then decides what should happen to the child or young person. If necessary, they may be placed with foster carers, a residential unit or in secure accommodation. The aim is to meet the needs of the child in the best possible way.

? **Web help**

Youth Justice Board in England and Wales

www.gov.uk/government/organisations/youth-justice-board-for-england-and-wales

Children's courts in Scotland and Northern Ireland

Scotland has a Children's Hearings System:
www.chscotland.gov.uk

Northern Ireland has a Youth Conferencing System:
www.youthjusticeagencyni.gov.uk

Civil courts

County Courts

County Courts deal with civil disputes, such as disagreements between landlords and tenants, personal injury claims or disputes arising from faulty goods. In Scotland, most of these are dealt with in the Sheriff Court. More serious civil cases are dealt with in Scotland's supreme civil court, the Court of Session, in Edinburgh.

The Small Claims Courts

In some cases you may want to take action against someone who owes you money and is refusing to pay. This is usually known as taking someone to the Small Claims Court. This court deals with people who are in dispute over relatively small amounts of money. The maximum claim limit varies in courts across England, Scotland, Wales and Northern Ireland so make sure you know how much it is before you start the small claims process.

Unlike Crown Courts, the hearing is held in an ordinary room with a judge and people from both sides sitting around a table.

HM Courts and Tribunal Service allows claimants and defendants to issue or respond to a money claim online. See **www.moneyclaim.gov.uk** for more information.

 **Web help**

Small Claims Courts

You can get more details about the small claims procedure from your local County Court or Sheriff Court. Details of your local court can be found at:

- England and Wales: **https://courttribunalfinder.service.gov.uk/**
- Scotland: **www.scotcourts.gov.uk**
- Northern Ireland: **www.courtsni.gov.uk**

Legal advice and aid

Solicitors

Solicitors can help you with legal problems. They are trained lawyers who give advice and may represent you in the lower courts. Some solicitors are qualified to represent clients in the higher courts as well. Solicitors have different areas of expertise, so it is important that you check that they have the right skills to represent you.

Solicitors' charges are usually based on how much time they spend on a case. It is very important to find out at the start how much a case is likely to cost.

 **Web help**

Finding a solicitor

The Citizens Advice Bureau: **www.citizensadvice.org.uk**

The Law Society: **www.lawsociety.org.uk**

Community Legal Advice: **http://find-legal-advice.justice.gov.uk/**

Legal aid

If you are questioned or charged with a crime you are entitled to free advice from a duty solicitor and free representation by a solicitor for your first appearance in court. You may get help with costs for further appearances in court, although this depends on the type of case and your income and savings. A solicitor can give information and advice on this.

Solicitors can also give information on schemes to cover the cost of their advice. Not all types of cases are covered by these schemes and the help available also depends on your income and savings.

'No win, no fee'

Sometimes the solicitor is paid on a 'no win, no fee' basis. In these cases the solicitor only charges you if they win the case. It is important to check all the possible costs before agreeing that a solicitor take the case on this basis – this is because you may need to pay the legal expenses of the other side (which may be expensive).

> ### ? Web help
>
> **Financial help for legal costs**
>
> - England and Wales: **www.gov.uk/legal-aid**
> - Scotland: **www.slab.org.uk**
> - Northern Ireland: **www.nilsc.org.uk**

Other legal help

There are a number of organisations that will help with civil cases.

> ### ? Web help
>
> - Law centres: **www.lawcentres.org.uk**
> - Citizens Advice Bureau: **www.adviceguide.org.uk**

Victims of crime

If you are victim of crime, you should contact the police first. The police can advise you about what to do next and keep you up to date as your case progresses. If you are a victim of a violent crime you can apply to the Criminal Injuries Compensation Authority for compensation. The crime must be reported to the police as quickly as possible and the application for compensation must be made within two years.

> ### ? Web help
>
> **Victims of crime**
>
> The Criminal Injuries Compensation Authority deals with claims in England, Wales and Scotland: **www.cica.gov.uk**
>
> The Compensation Agency deals with Northern Ireland: **www.dojni.gov.uk/compensation-agency**
>
> Victim Support: **www.victimsupport.org.uk**

Chapter 2

Working life

In this chapter you will learn about:

- Employment
- Setting up a business
- Your rights and responsibilities
- Taxes and benefits

The world of work

About three-quarters of jobs in the UK are in the service sector. This sector includes a wide range of jobs that offer a particular service, from solicitors to refuse collectors. As technology develops, the range of jobs available changes too.

Finding a job

First, you need to check that you are allowed to work in the UK. The Home Office can give you information about this if you are not sure. Employers must check that people who work for them have a legal right to work in the UK.

Jobcentre Plus is run by the Department for Work and Pensions, which is a government department. Trained staff there can help you apply for jobs or claim benefits. They also arrange interpreters.

Universal Jobmatch is an online service that is supported by the government. You can use it to search for and apply for jobs.

Jobs are also advertised in newspapers, on the internet, in employment agencies, on supermarket notice boards and in shop windows. Companies often show vacancies on their websites.

[?] **Web help**

Finding a job

Check whether you are allowed to work:
www.gov.uk/legal-right-work-uk

Universal Jobmatch: **www.gov.uk/jobsearch**

Qualifications and training

Jobs often need special qualifications. You may have studied to obtain qualifications in another country and will need to check whether these are accepted in the UK.

If you want to improve your chances of getting a job, further qualifications may be useful. Some employers may offer training, and many courses (including English) are available at your local college, although there may be a fee for these courses. Finding voluntary work can also help you gather useful skills and experience to help with job applications.

[?] **Web help**

Qualifications

Check your qualifications with the National Academic Recognition Information Centre (NARIC):
http://ecctis.co.uk/naric

Applying for a job

When you are looking for a job, you will often need a curriculum vitae (CV) to show an employer your skills and experience. It should not be too long – no more than two sides of A4 paper. Many organisations ask you to fill in an application form online, so you need to be prepared with all the relevant information before you start.

Employers usually provide a job description, so you need to make sure that your CV, application form and covering letter match the requirements of the job. You can usually do your application on a computer and submit it by email. You will also be asked for two referees who might be past employers or college tutors. It is important to tell the truth; if you don't, you might lose your job later.

The National Careers Service offers help with getting a job – from planning a career and writing CVs to telling you about your rights once you have the job.

? **Web help**

Writing a CV:

https://nationalcareersservice.direct.gov.uk

Interviews

If your application fits the job description you may be called for an interview. You should dress smartly, whatever the job. There may be a task to prepare for the interview and you should also think of some questions to ask about the job.

If the job involves working with children or vulnerable people, you will need a criminal record check (see web help for more information on this).

? **Web help**

Checks an employer can make:

https://www.gov.uk/employers-checks-job-applicants

> **!** **Action**
>
> **Find out the location of your nearest JobCentre Plus.**
>
> **Use the website to put together a CV.**
>
> **Look at jobs available on the Universal Jobmatch website.**

Rights and responsibilities at work

Once you have found a job, both you and your employer have legal responsibilities:

- **Employers** must pay employees for their work, treat them fairly and care for their health and safety.
- **Employees** should work with reasonable skill and care and follow reasonable instructions. They must not damage their employer's business. They should turn up for work on time and on the days that they have agreed to work, unless they are ill (in which case, they should try to inform their manager that they are unable to work on that day).

A written contract or statement

Once you accept a job your employer may give you a contract of employment to sign. The contract sets out the conditions of your employment as well as the employees' and the employers' rights and responsibilities towards one another. If you do not receive a contract of employment, you must receive a written statement of particulars in writing from your employer within two months of starting the job. This is not a contract itself but should describe the main terms of your employment.

The statement should set out:

- Your name and job title
- What you will be paid
- Your working hours
- How many days' holiday you will have each year
- Your pension (if your employer has a pension scheme)

- The period of notice to be given by you and your employer to end your employment
- Your employer's address
- The location of your place of work.

The contract and the written statement are very important – especially if there is a dispute.

Your employer must give you a pay slip showing how much you have been paid and how much is deducted for tax and National Insurance.

Paying income tax and National Insurance

People in the UK are liable to pay tax on their income. The money raised by taxes pays for government services such as roads, health, education, the police, the fire service and the armed forces.

Tax is usually taken directly from your pay by your employer. If you are self-employed, you must pay your own tax through the 'self-assessment' system. Sometimes you are sent a tax return asking about your income. You must fill it in honestly and return it.

Everyone below the state pension age who is working must also pay National Insurance Contributions. They are usually deducted in the same way as income tax. Self-employed people must pay these contributions themselves. If you do not make these payments you may not be able to claim benefits or receive a pension.

Every UK citizen is sent a National Insurance number as they approach the age of 16. If you have permission to work in the UK or are an asylum seeker with permission to stay, you should apply to Jobcentre Plus for a number if you do not yet have one. You will need evidence of identity and evidence that you are allowed to work. You can start work without a number but you must apply for one.

! Action

What does 'income' include'? Find out about how taxes are paid.

How does self-assessment work?

What benefits are affected if you do not pay National Insurance?

Responsibility for health and safety

The workplace must be safe and employers have a duty to ensure that it is. Employees have a legal duty to follow safety regulations and to work safely and responsibly. If you are worried about health and safety at your workplace, talk to your supervisor, manager or trade union representative. You need to follow the right procedures and your employer must not dismiss you or treat you unfairly for raising a concern.

> **? Web help**
>
> **Health and Safety Executive**
>
> You can find out about the standards required: **www.hse.gov.uk**

Trade unions

In the UK 6.5 million people belong to a trade union. They join because a trade union aims to improve pay and working conditions of its members. If you have problems at work, a trade union will often help you to deal with your employer.

You do not have to be a member of a union. It is your choice. An employer must accept union members in the workplace and treat you fairly – even if they do not negotiate with a union on terms such as pay and conditions.

You will pay a subscription as a union member. The money is used to:

- maintain the trade union's offices and facilities
- communicate with members
- produce publicity material for campaigns
- pay trade union staff.

If there is a union at your work then you will you usually pay for your membership by monthly subscription. This is either deducted from your pay and paid directly to the union or you can arrange a direct debit (automatic payment) from your bank account each month.

? **Web help**

Trade unions

Find out about trade unions in the UK: **www.tuc.org.uk**

! **Action**

Find out which trade union takes responsibility for your area of work.

Children and work

New mothers and fathers

As a new parent, you should be aware of your rights and responsibilities at work. These include:

- time off for antenatal care (a legal right)
- maternity leave (a legal right for full- and part-time employees)
- maternity pay (depends on how long you have been working for your employer)
- paternity leave (available if you've worked for at least 26 weeks for your employer)
- giving 15 weeks' notice of the date of birth (the father must also give at least 15 weeks' notice if they want paternity leave).

Working mothers and fathers enjoy certain rights, but also have responsibility for keeping their employers informed.

? **Web help**

Maternity benefits

Find out about your eligibility for maternity benefits:
https://www.gov.uk/maternity-pay-leave/overview

Children at work

There are strict laws about the work children can do. The general rule is that they are not allowed to work until the age of 13 – but there are exceptions, such as performing on the stage or in films and modelling. They will need a special licence to do this.

From 13 to 16 years old young people can only do light work on a part-time basis. They are not allowed to work in most pubs, betting shops or factories. Children who work usually have to get an employment permit from their local authority.

 Action

Find out how to claim maternity benefits.

Find out what the law says about the hours that children aged 13–16 are allowed to work.

Where should you go, in your local area, to get an employment permit for a child?

Problems in the workplace

A range of laws protect employees in the UK. If an employer breaks the law, employees have the right to take legal action against that employer.

Equal rights and discrimination

It is against the law for employers to discriminate against someone who works either part-time or full-time, on any of the following grounds:

- sex
- nationality, race, colour or ethnic group
- disability
- religion
- sexual orientation
- age.

In Northern Ireland, the law also bans discrimination on grounds of political opinion.

There are a few exceptions to these laws – for example, when the job involves working for someone in their own home.

 Action

Find out about the Equality Act 2010.

Sexual harassment

Sexual harassment can affect both men and women. It can take different forms including:

- indecent remarks
- the display of offensive or inappropriate material
- inappropriate comments about the way you look
- comments or questions about your sex life
- inappropriate touching or sexual demands
- bullying or being treated in a way that is rude, hostile, degrading or humiliating because of your sex

- decisions made in the workplace that are based on the acceptance or rejection of sexual demands.

If this happens to you, tell a friend, colleague or trade union representative and ask the person to stop. Keep a written record of what happened, and who may have seen or heard the harassment. If it doesn't stop, report it to your employer or trade union. Employers are responsible for the behaviour of their employees and should take action to deal with the problem.

[?] Web help

Dealing with discrimination

If you are not satisfied with your employer's response, you can ask for advice and support from:

- the Equality and Human Rights Commission: **www.equalityhumanrights.com**
- the Equality Commission for Northern Ireland: **www.equalityni.org**
- the Citizens Advice Bureau: **www.citizensadvice.org.uk**
- your trade union
- ACAS (the Advisory, Conciliation and Arbitration Service): **www.acas.org.uk**

Losing your job

You may lose your job if you fail to do it properly or break your contract in some way. You may also lose your job if your employer no longer needs you.

Dismissal

You can be dismissed immediately for gross misconduct. This includes things such as theft, physical violence, seriously neglecting your work or refusing to do as you are asked.

You can be dismissed if your employer claims you:

- cannot do your job properly
- are unacceptably late
- are absent from work without explanation.

Before dismissal you must be given a warning and the opportunity to improve. If things don't improve, you can be given notice to leave.

You cannot be dismissed unfairly. If your working life is made so difficult that you have to leave, you may get compensation. If you feel that you have been wrongly treated, you should take your case to an employment tribunal, which is a court that deals with issues at work. There will be a fee for doing this.

 **Web help**

Employment tribunals

You can find out more about employment tribunals on the gov.uk website at: **https://www.gov.uk/employment-tribunals**

Your trade union representative may also be able to help you.

Redundancy

You may be made redundant if the company no longer needs you or can't afford to pay you. You are normally legally entitled to redundancy pay – but only if you have been working for your employer for two years or more. The amount depends on how long you have been working for your employer and whether your employer has their own scheme. If you consider that you have been made redundant unfairly, you can apply to an employment tribunal.

Web help

Redundancy pay

You can find out more about redundancy pay here:
www.gov.uk/redundant-your-rights/redundancy-pay

Benefits

If you lose your job and fail to find another one, you may be entitled to some benefits while searching for employment. You must go to a Jobcentre Plus and 'sign on'. This involves being interviewed and completing forms to explain your skills. You must be able to show that you are searching for a job.

If your adviser at the Jobcentre Plus accepts your application, you may receive Jobseeker's Allowance, which is a sum of money paid to you every week to help you while you are looking for work.

If you have other people to support you may be entitled to other benefits too.

The social security system pays welfare benefits to people who do not have enough money to live on. Help may be available for the sick and disabled, older people, the unemployed and those on low incomes. Your adviser will explain the benefits you can claim.

If you do not have the legal rights of residence (or 'settlement') in the UK you cannot usually receive benefits. Arrangements for paying and receiving benefits are complicated because they have to take account of many different situations.

? Web help

Benefits while unemployed

Find out about Jobseeker's Allowance:
www.gov.uk/jobseekers-allowance

Find out about signing on: **www.gov.uk/contact-jobcentre-plus**

Pensions

Everyone in the UK will get a state pension provided by the government when they retire if they have paid enough National Insurance Contributions.

The state pension age is increasing and will depend on when you were born. For men born before 6 December 1953 the state pension age is 65. For women born before 6 April 1950 the state pension age is 60. It will increase to 65 for women by November 2018. After this it will gradually increase to 68 for both men and women.

Many people also receive a pension through their work and some also pay into a personal pension plan. If you meet certain conditions, you may be eligible for a workplace pension, which means your employer must make payments towards your pension.

？ Web help

Pensions

Check whether you are eligible for a workplace pension:
www.gov.uk/auto-enrolled-into-workplace-pension

You can use this calculator to work out at what age you would receive your pension and how much you might receive:
www.gov.uk/calculate-state-pension

> **Action**
>
> **Do you have a pension, apart from the state pension? Work out what you are likely to receive when you retire and decide whether you need any more.**

Working for yourself

You may want to set up a business and work for yourself. If so, you have three options. You can set up as a sole trader, in partnership or you can start a limited company. The type of visa you have will affect your ability to work for yourself.

> **? Web help**
>
> **Setting up a business**
>
> There is practical information about setting up a business here: **www.gov.uk/starting-up-a-business**

Becoming a sole trader

As a sole trader, you are self-employed – and running your business as an individual. Once you have paid your taxes, you can keep the remaining profit from your business. It is important to remember that if you choose to run your business as a sole trader, the law does not recognise any difference between your business finances and your personal finances. If your business owes money, then you will be liable for the debt.

You must register with HM Revenue & Customs (HMRC) and follow certain rules when naming your business and running it.

When you choose a name for your business you can use your own name or choose a business name but you must not:

- use terms that suggest your business's status, such as 'limited' or plc

- use a name which is too like another business or trademark in the same market
- suggest any connection with central or local government
- use words or expressions that have sensitive connections without permission
- be offensive.

You must always include your own name and business name, if you have one, on any business paperwork such as invoices and letters.

A sole trader can employ other people.

Once you have started business, you must register for self-assessment with HMRC.

As a sole trader you are responsible for the following:

- registering with HMRC to file a tax return through self-assessment
- sending a self-assessment tax return every year
- paying income tax on any profits your business makes
- paying any debts your business owes
- paying bills for anything you buy for your business, such as stock or equipment

- keeping accurate records of your business's sales and expenses
- paying National Insurance
- registering for value added tax (VAT) if the value of your total sales reaches the threshold.

[?] Web help

Sole traders

Find out more: **https://www.gov.uk/set-up-sole-trader**

What's the VAT limit?

www.hmrc.gov.uk/vat/start/register/when-to-register.htm

Setting up a business partnership

As a partner in a business you and other partners share responsibility for the business.

The partners share all the profits from the business between them. Each partner is then responsible for paying tax on their share.

Each partner is responsible for:

- losses made by the business
- paying for things bought for the business, such as stock or equipment.

A limited company counts as a legal person and can be a partner in a partnership.

When you set up a partnership, you must:

- choose a named partner who takes responsibility for keeping the records and dealing with tax returns. Whoever is chosen must register with HMRC – and will be registered for self-assessment tax.
- register other partners for self-assessment tax and National Insurance as soon as possible (once the business is up and running).

Tax responsibilities

As a partner in a business, you must:

- send a partnership self-assessment tax return every year
- send a personal self-assessment tax return every year
- pay income tax on your share of the partnership's profits
- pay National Insurance
- register for VAT if takings might reach the VAT limit in a year.

 **Web help**

Setting up a partnership

www.gov.uk/business-legal-structures/ordinary-business-partnership

---

In Scotland partnerships are different. They are known as firms and have a 'legal personality' separate from the individual partners.

? **Web help**

Scottish firms

Find out about the difference between partnerships in England and Wales and those in Scotland:
www.hmrc.gov.uk/manuals/ihtmanual/ihtm25091.htm

If you don't want to be personally responsible for a business's losses, you can set up a limited partnership or limited liability partnership.

- Partners in a limited liability partnership are only responsible for the amount they have invested.
- In a limited partnership, some partners have limited liability but others don't.

Apart from limited liability, partners have the same responsibilities as in ordinary partnerships. They are mainly set up by professionals such as solicitors and accountants.

[?] **Web help**

Limited liability partnerships

www.gov.uk/business-legal-structures/limited-partnership-and-limited-liability-partnership

---

Setting up a limited company

A limited company is legally separate from you as an individual. It can own property, incur debts, sue and be sued. Any business dealings are made on behalf of the company rather than yourself.

Setting up and running a limited company needs more legal administration than a sole trader business. The advantage is that your risk is limited to the amount you invested in the company and any guarantees you gave when raising finance for the business.

Limited companies pay corporation tax on their profits. Company directors are taxed as employees in the same way as any other people you employ to work for the company.

Registering your company

Your company must be registered with Companies House. To register you must have:

- a company name and registered address
- at least one director
- at least one shareholder
- details of the company's shares – known as the 'memorandum of association'
- rules about how the company is run – known as 'Articles of Association'.

How to register

You can register your company:

- online
- by post
- through an agent.

It is quicker and cheaper to do this online.

Company name
The name of your company must end in either 'Limited' or 'Ltd' and the name must not:

- be the same as any other name on the Companies House index of names
- contain a 'sensitive' word or expression, unless you get permission
- suggest a connection with government or local authorities
- be offensive.

If you have a trademark, it is not protected simply by registering your company. You must register trademarks separately.

? Web help

Registering your business

Companies House gives you all the information you need about registering your business: **www.companieshouse.gov.uk/ infoAndGuide/companyRegistration.shtml**

Registered address

Companies House needs a registered address for your company so official communications will reach you. It doesn't have to be the address of the business itself. It must be a physical (real) address and it must be in the country where the business operates. You can use your home address if it meets these rules.

Directors

The director, or directors, are legally responsible for running the company. You can make another company a director – but at least one of your company's directors must be an individual.

Directors must make sure that the company is run properly.

? **Web help**

Directors' responsibilities

https://www.gov.uk/running-a-limited-company/directors-responsibilities

---

Shareholders

Shareholders are the owners of the company and they have certain rights – such as agreeing to changes made by the company.

When you register a company, you must state:

- the number of shares
- the total value of the shares
- the names and addresses of all the shareholders.

Articles of Association

The Articles of Association are agreed by the shareholders and directors. They set out the rules for running the company.

You can write your own, but most people use the model you can find online.

[**?**] **Web help**

Articles of Association

www.gov.uk/limited-company-formation/articles-of-association

Your company and corporation tax

A company must pay corporation tax on any taxable profits. To do this, you must tell HMRC that you have started trading. You will receive a unique taxpayer reference and will be asked some specific details about your company. This will allow them to work out when your tax will be due.

Starting to trade means carrying out any business activity including buying, selling, employing someone, advertising or renting a property.

HMRC will want answers to the following questions:

- When did you start your business?
- What is your company name and registered number?
- What is the main address where you do business?
- What kind of business do you do?
- On what date do you make up your annual accounts?
- Have you taken over a business or are you part of a group?

[**?**] **Web help**

Setting up a company

There is much more information about how to set up a company and what documents are needed here:
www.gov.uk/limited-company-formation

Chapter 3

Everyday life

In this chapter you will learn about:

- Language
- Money
- Shopping
- Housing

Language in the UK

The English language is a great mixture of languages from all over the world. There are strong links with European and Scandinavian languages, but some English words originate in places as far away as India, Africa and many other countries and regions. Here are some examples:

- Indian – pyjamas, shampoo, mugger and bungalow
- Arabic – alcohol, giraffe, candy and chemistry
- African – jazz, jamboree, banjo and zombie
- Chinese – tea, typhoon, silk and tycoon.

Everyone in the UK speaks English but there are also regional languages and dialects.

- Welsh is taught in schools in Wales.
- Some people in Scotland and Northern Ireland speak Gaelic.
- Cornish is a recognised language spoken by some people in Cornwall.

People in different parts of the country speak with different dialects and accents. If you are not used to a local accent, you have to listen carefully to what is being said.

- In Liverpool you may hear people speaking Scouse.
- In Tyneside (the Newcastle area) you may hear people speaking Geordie.
- In parts of London, you may hear people speaking Cockney.

> **[!] Action**
>
> **What local languages and dialects can be heard where you live?**

Looking after your money

The UK currency

In the UK we use pounds and pence. The pound is divided into 100 pence. It is a decimal currency so everything is counted in 10s – which makes the sums easy!

Coins are of the following values:

1p	2p	5p	10p

20p	50p	£1	£2

Notes are of the following values: £5, £10, £20 and £50.

Northern Ireland and Scotland have the same pounds and pence but have Northern Irish and Scottish bank notes. They are valid everywhere but do not have to be accepted in shops.

If you want to change a different currency into pounds – or the other way round – there are plenty of choices. Banks, building societies, post offices and bureaux de change will all get foreign currencies for you. You can also do it online. Some currencies have to be ordered in advance but you can usually get euros and US dollars immediately. Exchange rates vary daily and you should check different places to find the best value.

Keeping your money safe

Most adults in the UK have an account at a bank or building society. Parents often open accounts for their children to help teach them about how to look after their money.

You need to prove who you are and where you live to open an account. Documents such as a passport, immigration document, or driving licence show who you are. A tenancy agreement or household bill proves where you live.

You can manage your account in the branch, on the telephone or by using the internet.

Employers usually pay wages straight into your account. It is then easy to arrange for the payment of regular and other bills from the account. If you are saving money, you will need to compare the banks and building societies to find out which will give you the best rate of interest.

[?] **Web help**

Choosing a bank account

Banks in the UK offer a range of different accounts and services, so it is important to find the one that meets your needs. There are several websites that can help you choose:

www.moneyadviceservice.org.uk
www.which.co.uk/money

A **cash card** allows you to use cash machines to withdraw money from your account. The bank will give you a personal identification number (PIN), which you must key in every time you use a machine. You need to keep this number secret.

A **debit card** allows you to pay for things without using cash. You must have enough money in your account to cover what you buy. If you lose your cash card or debit card you must tell the bank immediately.

⊡ Action

Find out which banks or building societies have a branch near you. Have a look online to see how their bank accounts compare.

Proving your identity

You may need to prove your identity to open a bank account, rent accommodation, enrol on a college course, hire a car, apply for benefits or get a marriage certificate. UK citizens do not have to carry identity (ID) cards.

Different organisations may ask for different documents as proof of identity.

⊡ Action

What documents can you use to prove your identity to open a bank account?

Borrowing money

If you borrow money you must be careful.

Check that:

- the lender is reputable and licensed
- you understand the terms and conditions

- the interest rate is competitive (not too high compared with the banks)
- you know the amount you will have to repay
- you can afford the repayments.

In the UK it is very common for people to borrow money when making big purchases. If you want to buy a house, you may need a mortgage. There is more information about buying houses in Chapter 4.

It is very important to make sure you don't borrow more than you can repay. You might borrow from a bank or building society or use a credit card.

Credit cards can be used to buy things in shops, on the telephone and using the internet.

A **store card** is like a credit card but can only be used in a specific shop.

If you use credit or store cards you will be sent a bill every month. If you do not pay the total amount on the bill you are charged interest, which may be very high. It is important to repay the money so you do not get into debt. If you lose your credit or store card you must report it to your lender straight away.

Sometimes fraud can take place with credit cards. If you find items on your statement that you haven't bought, you need to call the credit card company immediately. They will usually refund the money that was taken.

Credit unions are financial cooperatives that are owned and controlled by their members. The members pool their savings and then make loans from this pool. Interest rates are usually lower than the ones at banks and building societies.

Being refused credit

Banks want to know all about you before they lend you money because they want to be sure that you are able to repay it. You may be refused credit if you do not match their requirements, so it is important to ensure that you have given them the correct information. If you are refused, ask why.

A refusal can depend on your credit rating. This is a measure of how reliable you are likely to be when repaying money. You can check your own credit rating online.

 Web help

Check your credit rating

www.experian.co.uk
www.equifax.co.uk

Action

Find out:

- about interest rates on savings.
- what interest rates credit cards charge if you do not repay the full amount each month.

The Ombudsman

If you feel you have been badly treated by any financial organisation, first try to sort the problem out with the company yourself. You can refer the matter to the Financial Ombudsman if it is still unresolved.

> **[?]** Web help
>
> **The Financial Ombudsman**
>
> www.financial-ombudsman.org.uk

Shopping

Protecting the consumer

When you buy something from a shop it must, by law, do everything you can reasonably expect and all that the seller and manufacturer claim.

The Sale of Goods Act 1979 states that when you buy anything from a shop or trader it must:

- be of satisfactory quality
- match the description
- be fit for purpose.

Shopping is one of the main leisure activities in the UK

Satisfactory quality

Being of 'satisfactory quality' means that your purchases must be free from faults, scratches or damage. They should also last for a reasonable length of time.

For example, a washing machine should wash clothes thoroughly and not leak water. It should continue to work for several years with normal use (although the guarantees often last only a year).

This rule applies to any goods you buy from a shop or trader, new or second-hand. It does not apply to anything bought privately from an individual. You need to be very careful when buying things from an advert in a newspaper or a card in a shop window – you need to check the item carefully before you agree to buy it.

Occasionally you might accept an item with a fault if you don't think it's a big problem. The sales assistant might have told you about a fault or you might have noticed it yourself. Sometimes, the shop will agree to sell you the item at a lower price ('at a discount').

Match the description

'Matching the description' means that anything you buy must be the same as the description on the packaging or advertisement at the time of sale. If you buy a tablet computer that says the battery lasts for six hours, it must last at least that long.

This rule applies to everything sold. Second-hand goods sold privately are included in this rule.

Fit for purpose

Being 'fit for purpose' means that any item you buy must do everything that is claimed by the seller on the packaging and advertising. Computer printers, for example, often have many other features, such as scanning and photocopying – if the box says the printer can photocopy a document then it must be able to do that. When you buy anything, the features described in the advertising should:

- be included in the product
- deliver efficient performance.

Taking care with your purchases

Sometimes you find problems with things you have bought from shops, by mail order or on the internet. Here are some things you can do to protect yourself if disputes arise:

- Be cautious of advertisements which make bold claims about what a product can do.
- Be cautious of people who try to sell you things at your door.
- Keep receipts as proof of purchase, especially if the goods were expensive.
- If there is a problem with something you bought, stop using it straight away and tell the shop or trader about the problem.
- If you have to make a complaint to a shop or company, keep a record of telephone calls and make a copy of any letters or emails that you send.

Prices are usually clearly marked on most new goods and these are the prices that customers should expect to pay. In general, people in the UK do not barter or negotiate prices for goods. Bargaining often does take place when buying houses, cars, second-hand items, and for some household services such as decorating or gardening.

Mail order and internet shopping

There are special regulations to protect people who buy goods from home, by post, phone or on the internet. As well as the rights listed above, you are entitled to cancel your order within seven working days if you decide that you do not want to buy the item. This does not apply to all purchases. For example, you cannot change your mind for tickets (for a football match for example) or accommodation bookings, audio and video recordings that have been opened, newspapers and magazines, and perishable items such as flowers or food.

You are also entitled to a full refund if you do not receive the goods by the date agreed or within 30 days if you did not agree a date.

If you are buying goods on the internet, it is important to make sure that you have the trader's full address. You also need to make sure that the website offers a secure way of paying.

Complaints

If a fault appears soon after you have bought an item and you are not responsible, you are entitled either to your money back or to a replacement. It is the shop's responsibility to deal with the problem.

If an item worked well at first and then developed a fault, you may still be entitled to all or some of your money back, to be offered a replacement or to have the item repaired free of charge. The action taken will depend on how long you have had the goods, how serious the fault is and whether it is unreasonable for a fault to have developed so soon.

Paying by credit card

If you have used a credit card to buy something which cost between £100 and £30,000 and there is a problem with it, you can claim the money back from the credit card company. This can be useful if the trader does not help to solve the problem or has gone out of business.

[?] Web help

Consumer protection

Trading Standards Office: **www.tradingstandards.gov.uk**

Citizens Advice Bureau: **www.citizensadvice.org.uk**

Consumers' Association: **www.which.co.uk**
This is a subscription service.

Services

The law covering services, such as hairdressing or shoe repairs, states that services must be done:

- with reasonable care and skill
- within a reasonable time
- for a reasonable charge.

To avoid problems it is a good idea to agree the price and exactly what you want to be done before the work starts.

Housing

Buying a
house

The costs of
running your
home

Renting a
house

Homelessness

Neighbours
(see Chapter 5)

Buying a house

In the UK most people use an estate agent to buy a home. You will
find them on every high street and most have websites designed to
help you in your search. It is important to remember that an estate
agent is working for the seller of the property. When you negotiate
the price, the agent has a duty to get the best price for the seller so
you must always be careful.

You can also buy a home at an auction but you need to be sure that
you have the money ready on the day. In Scotland, you can find
out about properties for sale from solicitors. The method of selling
houses in Scotland is not the same as in the other parts of the UK.
Once you have made an offer on a property in Scotland and it has
been accepted, you have entered a legally binding contract and
neither side can easily withdraw.

Most people borrow money from a bank or building society to buy a
home. The loan is called a mortgage and is usually paid back over a
long time (for example, 25 years). You will pay interest so it is worth

looking for a good deal. The amount you can borrow will depend on your income and the size of deposit you can put down. There are different sorts of mortgage such as trackers or fixed rate. You must work out the type that suits you best. Lenders also charge arrangement fees – so expect some extra costs and ask the lender how much they will be. This all needs to be sorted out before you make an offer so you know exactly how much you can afford to pay each month.

You will need to appoint a solicitor or licensed conveyancer to carry out the legal work involved. It is important to check the fee before you tell them to go ahead.

It is important to pay your mortgage every month. If you don't the house may be repossessed and sold so the lender can get their money back. You must also carry out any repairs that are necessary.

[?] **Web help**

Finding a solicitor

You can find a solicitor near you: **http://solicitors.lawsociety.org.uk**

Buying a house in Scotland

www.adviceguide.org.uk/scotland/housing_s/housing_buying_and_selling_s/buying_a_home_scotland.htm

---

Most people use an estate agent to buy a home. You can often see their signs outside houses that are for sale.

> ### ! Action
>
> **How does a bank or building society decide whether to give you a mortgage?**
>
> **Find out about solicitors and licensed conveyancers in your area.**

Renting a house

You can rent a house from the council, a housing association or a private landlord. There is a shortage of council housing in many areas and waiting lists can be long. You will be assessed on need, which will be greater if you have children, are ill or homeless. Your eligibility for housing may depend on your immigration status.

Shared ownership is available through some housing associations. You buy part of your home and pay rent for the rest. It can be useful if you can't afford to buy the whole property.

Many people rent in the private sector. When you have found somewhere you would like to live, you will be asked to sign a tenancy agreement and pay a deposit. You should read the agreement carefully so you know about the responsibilities involved. The deposit should be returned when you leave if you haven't done any damage.

The rent will be fixed when you sign the contract. This cannot be raised and must be paid until the contract runs out. At the end of the contract, your landlord may decide to increase the rent.

As a tenant, you have both rights and responsibilities.

Your rights

As a tenant, you have the right to:

- a written or oral contract or tenancy agreement that is fair and complies with the law
- know who your landlord is
- see an energy performance certificate for the property
- live in the property undisturbed
- live in a property that's safe and in a good state of repair
- challenge unreasonably high charges
- be protected from unfair eviction (being told to leave) and unfair rent
- have your deposit returned when the tenancy ends – and have it protected
- a written agreement if you have a fixed-term tenancy of more than three years.

If you don't know who your landlord is, ask the person or company you pay rent to, in writing. If they don't give you this information within 21 days, your landlord may be fined.

Your responsibilities

When you agree to a tenancy, you have responsibilities as well as rights.

- **Always pay the agreed rent**
  If you are in dispute with the landlord or the property requires repairs, you must still pay the rent or you will be in breach of your tenancy agreement.
- **Take care of the property**
  Close the windows so the rain can't get in. Leave some heating on low if you're away in cold weather to prevent the pipes from bursting.
- **Pay the bills as agreed with the landlord**
  You will probably have to pay council tax and utility bills.
- **Give your landlord access to the property**
  Your landlord must give you at least 24 hours' notice and arrange

a reasonable time of day to inspect it or carry out repairs. If there is an emergency, the landlord has the right to immediate access.

- **Pay for repairs if you cause any damage**
  This includes damage done by friends and family.

- **Do not sublet your property**
  You can only sublet a property if the tenancy agreement, or your landlord, allows it.

If you don't carry out these responsibilities, your landlord has the right to take legal action to evict you.

The landlord's responsibilities
Your landlord's main responsibilities include:

- giving you their name and address or that of their agent
- providing you with a statement of tenancy terms
- recording rent payments
- providing you with an energy performance certificate for your property
- respecting your right to peace and quiet in your home
- ensuring gas, electricity and furniture safety requirements are met in your home
- maintaining the structure and outside of the property
- giving you at least 24 hours' notice before accessing the property to carry out repairs, except in case of an emergency
- following the correct legal procedures if they want you to leave the property.

The costs of running your home
Water
Your water is supplied by a water company. You pay for your water either monthly, six-monthly or annually. Many houses now have water meters which show exactly how much water has been used. These meters are read by the water company.

Electricity and gas
All homes have electricity and most have gas. Gas may not be available if you live in a rural area. You can choose between different

gas and electricity suppliers. They have different prices and terms and conditions so you have to select the one that suits you best. The company may want you to read your own meter and send them the information.

Telephone

Most homes already have a telephone line, which is often known as a landline. If you need a new line, contact a telephone service provider or a cable company. Many companies offer landline, mobile phone and broadband internet services.

Council tax

Council tax or rates pay for your local services. The amount you pay depends on the size of your home. If you are on benefits you may pay less. If you live on your own you pay 25% less, apart from in Northern Ireland.

Council tax pays for a range of services including refuse collection. Refuse is usually collected every week but different areas have different systems. Households are usually asked to use a separate bin for waste that can be recycled. This may not be collected at the same time as the other waste.

Buildings and household contents insurance

Buildings insurance

A home with a mortgage must be insured against damage to the building caused, for example, by fire, burst water pipes or a falling tree. This insurance usually covers accidental damage to 'fixtures and fittings' (such as washbasins and fitted cupboards) as well. The landlord arranges this insurance for rented buildings.

Household contents insurance

Many companies sell this type of insurance. If you own a house or have property in a house, it is wise to insure your possessions against theft or damage. You can often add 'personal possessions cover' to insure against loss or theft of items when you are out and about or travelling abroad. People often buy insurance on the internet or over the telephone.

Action

Work out what insurance you need for yourself and your possessions.

? Web help

Water companies

Find out which water companies provide water in your area:
www.ofwat.gov.uk/consumerissues/watercompanies/map/

! Action

Find out how to pay your council tax.

Does council tax cover all the costs of local services?

Find out how to contact the police and emergency services.

Find out how refuse is dealt with in your area.

Homelessness

If you have nowhere to live, you are officially described as being homeless. You should go to the local authority in England, Wales or Scotland for help. In Northern Ireland go to the Housing Executive. They do not have a duty to house you unless you meet certain criteria.

You can also get help from Shelter, a housing advice charity that offers help to people who are homeless. They can tell you if you are entitled to help if you become homeless and help with other housing issues, such as problems with landlords.

Chapter 4

Family life

In this chapter you will learn about:

- Your rights and responsibilities to your family
- Marriage
- Health
- Education

Your rights and responsibilities to your family

Everyone in the UK has a right to respect for their family life, providing they don't break the law or have a negative effect on others. Our human rights are protected by the Human Rights Act which includes:

- freedom of belief and religion
- freedom of speech
- freedom to belong to organisations such as trade unions
- a right not to be discriminated against
- a right for men and women to be treated equally
- a right to an education
- a right to privacy
- a right to a fair trial
- a right to join in the election of a government.

These rights come with equally important responsibilities. Among these are:

- a responsibility to respect and obey the law
- a responsibility to respect the rights of others, including their right to their own opinions
- a responsibility to treat others with fairness
- a responsibility to look after yourself and your family
- a responsibility to look after the area in which you live and the environment.

These rights and responsibilities influence and affect the way families work. As a member of a family you have responsibilities to the rest of your family, your neighbours and other people around you.

Marriage and civil partnership

Many people decide to make their relationship official by getting married or making a civil partnership.

Key points to consider

Before marrying or entering a civil partnership, you should consider the following points:

- You must be 16 years old or older.
- At 16 and 17 you need parents' permission everywhere but Scotland.
- You can't marry close blood relatives, but marriage between first cousins is legally permitted.
- You can get married in a place of worship, a register office or a licensed venue.
- Same-sex couples can mark their relationship with a civil partnership or by marriage in a civil ceremony.
- Couples need their birth certificates or personal identity documents to get a marriage certificate.
- People who have been married or had a civil partner before must show proof that the relationship has legally ended.
- A woman often takes her husband's surname when they get married (but she doesn't have to).

Before your marriage or civil partnership

To get married at a register office in the UK, you must give at least 16 days' notice before the ceremony can take place. The notice will be displayed to the public for 15 days at the register office. You must have lived in the registration district of the office for at least the seven days before the ceremony. To sort out your plans, you need to contact your local register office.

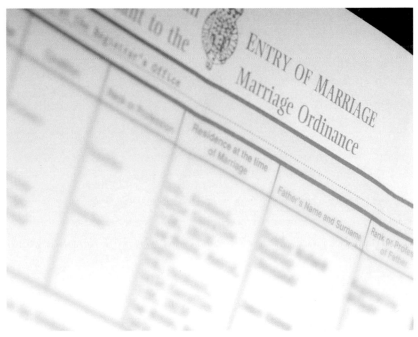

A paper marriage certificate looks like this

If you are from Switzerland, the European Economic Area (EEA) or are under immigration control, you must go to a designated register office.

[?] Web help

Register offices

To find out the location of your local register office:
www.gov.uk/marriages-civil-partnerships/giving-notice-at-your-local-register-office

To find out the location of a designated register office:
www.gov.uk/government/publications/designated-register-offices-in-england-and-wales

---

> **! Action**
>
> **Find out how the process in Scotland and Northern Ireland differs from that in England and Wales.**

If you are coming from another country and planning to get married or enter into a civil partnership, you must have permission to be in the UK.

- If your future spouse or civil partner is a British citizen or is settled here, you will need a visa.
- If you are from outside the EEA and your future spouse or civil partner is from the EEA or Switzerland – but not the UK – you will need an EEA family permit.
- If you and your future spouse or civil partner are from outside the EEA or Switzerland and you want to hold the marriage ceremony in the UK, you will need a Marriage Visitor visa. You must then leave the country within six months.

If you come to the UK to get married, you must do so within a year of your arrival or within three months if you're in Scotland.

You may be able to give notice of your marriage ceremony if you are living outside the UK. Some countries have a special agreement, called the British Subjects Facilities Acts. To do this you must both be UK or Commonwealth citizens, and one of you must be a resident of England or Wales.

> **? Web help**
>
> **Marriage/civil partnership permission**
>
> Visas: **www.gov.uk/remain-in-uk-family**
>
> EEA family permit: **www.gov.uk/family-permit**
>
> Marriage Visitor visa: **www.gov.uk/marriage-visa**
>
> British Subject Facilities Acts:
> **www.gov.uk/marriages-civil-partnerships/what-you-need-to-do**

Giving notice at the register office

You will need to give proof of your name, age and nationality so you need at least two of the following documents:

- passport
- birth certificate
- driving licence
- national identity card
- immigration status document.

You will also need to show evidence of where you live. This might be your driving licence or a:

- bank statement
- council tax bill
- gas, water or electricity bill.

Any of these must be dated within the last three months.

You will also have to pay the fee for the ceremony when you give notice.

If you are widowed or divorced you need to take either:

- your decree absolute or final order, or
- the death certificate of your former partner.

If you were divorced in another country, the divorce will usually be recognised, providing it was legal where it took place. The registrar will look at the documents and may decide to check their validity before going ahead.

Religious ceremonies

If you want to have a religious ceremony, it can be held at a church, chapel or other registered religious building. You can have a religious blessing after a civil ceremony in a register office if you wish.

As a same-sex couple, you can't get married in an Anglican church but you can get married in other religious buildings if the building has been registered for the marriage of same-sex couples and the rules of the religion allow same-sex marriages.

Anglican marriages

To get married in your local church, you usually have to have the 'banns' read at a Sunday service for three weeks. You don't usually need to give notice with the register office. Officials performing Anglican marriages will register your marriage. This is also the case for marriages in a Catholic church or the churches of other Christian denominations.

Jewish and Quaker marriages

You must give at least 16 days' notice at the register office before the ceremony. The officials who perform the marriage will register it for you.

Marriages in all other religions

You must give notice of the ceremony at the register office at least 16 days before the event. If the minister or priest has been authorised to register marriages then you don't need to do this.

You will need to have a civil ceremony as well, or have a registrar in attendance, if the official who performs the ceremony is not authorised to register marriages.

At the ceremony

If you are getting married, you must exchange vows. These are formal words that commit you to each other. You may want to have some other wording as well. This should all be discussed with the person performing the ceremony at some time before the event.

At the ceremony for civil partners, you don't need to exchange vows but you can do so if you wish. You can also have readings, music and songs but none of it must be religious.

Your wedding or civil partnership must be witnessed by at least two people.

The register must be signed by you and your spouse or partner and your two witnesses.

What does it cost?

There are fees for registering a marriage or civil partnership in the UK. There is a basic fee for a simple event but register offices usually offer packages at different prices. Some of the more expensive options may include luxury rooms that hold larger numbers of guests.

There is a small fee for a marriage or civil partnership certificate. You will probably need a copy of the certificate to prove your marital status in the future.

Other venues

You can be married or become civil partners in all register offices but there are all sorts of other venues where you can hold your ceremony. You can even get married in caves in Edinburgh or on the London Eye.

All venues must be approved by the local council.

> ### ? Web help
>
> **Wedding venues**
>
> Find out where you can hold your ceremony:
> **https://www.gov.uk/government/publications/civil-marriages-and-partnerships-approved-premises-list**

Living together

If you and your partner live together you do not have the same rights as people who are married or have a civil partnership. For example, you have no right to:

- a share of a house if you do not own a share
- a tenancy unless your name is on the contract
- a share of the estate on death unless it is stated in their will.

If you have children, both of you are responsible for supporting them until they are 18.

Forced marriage

In the UK you cannot be forced to marry if you don't want to. Marriages can be arranged but both people must agree. Registrars, who carry out civil weddings, are trained to look out for situations where they feel that either the bride or groom does not want to get married.

If you do not wish to be married, then you (or someone representing you) can apply for a court order to prevent the wedding taking place. The order will also protect you from the people who wanted to force you to get married. Anyone breaking the order can be sent to prison for two years.

In 2008 the Forced Marriage Protection Orders, which allow these court orders to be enforced, were introduced for England, Wales and Northern Ireland. In 2011 similar Protection Orders were introduced in Scotland.

Domestic violence and abuse

If you are violent or abusive towards your partner, whether they are male or female, you are committing a serious offence.

If you are being abused, there are several places to get help. The Citizens Advice Bureau or a solicitor will be able suggest organisations in your area.

- The National Domestic Violence Helpline has a free phone number on **0808 2000 247**. It will help you whether you are male or female.
- There are shelters and refuges in some areas which offer you a safe place to stay if you've been subjected to violence.
- The police can find you a safe place to stay.
- There are organisations such as Mankind which will give you guidance.
- You can find helpful contacts in the *Yellow Pages*.

[?] Web help

To find out more about forced marriage and domestic violence, visit:

www.gov.uk/forced-marriage

www.nationaldomesticviolencehelpline.org.uk

www.mankind.org.uk

Divorce and ending a civil partnership

You must prove to a court that your marriage or civil partnership has 'irretrievably broken down' before they will grant you a divorce or end your partnership. This cannot take place until you have been married for a year. There are a number of ways to prove that a marriage or civil partnership has broken down.

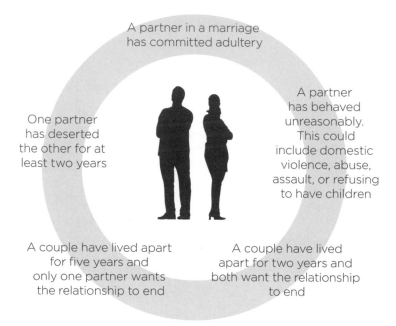

A partner in a marriage has committed adultery

A partner has behaved unreasonably. This could include domestic violence, abuse, assault, or refusing to have children

One partner has deserted the other for at least two years

A couple have lived apart for five years and only one partner wants the relationship to end

A couple have lived apart for two years and both want the relationship to end

Causes of breakdown

Getting help

When a marriage or civil partnership breaks down, there can be a lot of stress for one or both people. Your family doctors may help by making an appointment with a family therapist. There are also charitable organisations which offer help in such circumstances.

If you have young children, or if there are problems over money or property, you must get advice from a solicitor.

[?] **Web help**

Relationship breakdown

For help in different parts of the UK, contact one of the following charitable organisations.

Relate in England and Wales: **www.relate.org.uk**

Relationships Scotland: **www.relationships-scotland.org.uk**

Relate Northern Ireland: **www.relateni.org**

Looking after your children

Parents who are married to one another have equal responsibility for their child or children until they reach the age of 18. Even if they separate or divorce, they still have joint responsibility.

If the parents are not married, only the mother has parental responsibility unless:

- both mother and father jointly register the child's birth
- the father marries the mother at a later date
- the mother agrees to equal parental responsibility
- the father acquires parental responsibility by applying to court.

If you are the civil partner or spouse but not the child's biological parent, you can have parental responsibility for your partner's child through the courts or by adopting them.

Financial responsibility

You have a responsibility to look after your children financially, whether or not you are married. Even if a father or mother does not have parental responsibility by law, they still have to support their children financially while they are:

- under the age of 16
- under 20 and in full-time education up to A-level or equivalent
- under 20 and the parent they live with gets Child Benefit for them.

The Child Maintenance Service will work out and collect the money when parents are separated or divorced.

? **Web help**

Child maintenance

Find out more about using the Child Maintenance Service:
www.gov.uk/child-maintenance

Control

As a parent, you are responsible for looking after your children until they are 18.

You can, by law, use reasonable force to discipline them. Smacking or 'reasonable chastisement' is acceptable in the eyes of the law, although it is discouraged. If you go too far, you will be prosecuted for assault. Any smack or punishment that leaves clear marks, welts, bruises or scratches is a prosecutable offence and you could face up to five years in jail. Your child may be taken into the care of the local authority.

Many voluntary organisations and local authorities offer parenting courses as well as support and advice on being a parent. There are also organisations which will help you if you need to discuss problems with bringing up children.

? Web help

Parenting

If you are in need of support contact: **http://familylives.org.uk**

Find a parenting course near you:
www.parentinguk.org/parent-portal/parenting-courses

Protecting children

Children have the right to protection if they are in danger. Local authorities have a legal duty to make sure that children come to no harm. The interests of the child must come first. The local authority will try to work with the family, but if there are still safety concerns the child may be moved to a children's home or put into the care of foster parents.

This is only done in an emergency or when all other options have failed.

[?] Web help

Child protection

The NSPCC listens to anyone who has concerns about a child: **www.nspcc.org.uk** or phone them on **0808 800 5000**.

Children and young people can contact ChildLine: **www.childline.org.uk** or call them on **0800 1111**.

Medical advice and treatment for children and young people

If your children are younger than 16 years old, you are responsible for their medical care. You will need to sign consent forms for any surgery. Once they are 16, as long as the nurse or doctor feels sure that they understand what is involved, they do not need parental consent.

Contraceptive advice and treatment is available to girls under the age of 16 if the doctor thinks that they understand the issues. The doctor will usually encourage the young person to talk to her parents.

Leaving children on their own

There is no law against leaving your children alone at home when they are younger than 16. You are trusted to use common sense in deciding whether a child younger than this will be safe on their own. If something goes wrong, however, you may be held responsible for not looking after them properly.

You will find childminders and nurseries everywhere across the country. They must all be must be registered and inspected by the Office for Standards in Education (Ofsted).

[?] Web help

Childminders and nurseries

You can search for childcare near you at: **www.gov.uk/find-registered-childminder**

You can search for a nursery near you at: **www.gov.uk/find-nursery-school-place**

Health

If you need health care in the UK, its cost depends on your status. As an immigrant, you may have to pay towards the cost of National Health Service (NHS) care. Some people take out insurance to pay for private health care. As a permanent resident, most services are free.

People have to pay for services such as eye tests, dental treatment and prescriptions for medicines. You do not have to pay for some of these services if they are for children, people over 60, pregnant women, those on low incomes and people with certain illnesses. Charges for services vary in different parts of the UK.

You can choose to pay for health care if you wish to have treatment in a private hospital. There are also some services that you can't usually get from the NHS, such as reflexology, osteopathy and acupuncture. You have to pay for these yourself.

People who use private health care pay for it themselves or with private health insurance.

? Web help

Health care

You can find out more about health care where you are:

England: **www.nhs.uk**

Scotland: **www.show.scot.nhs.uk**

Wales: **www.wales.nhs.uk**

Northern Ireland: **www.hscni.net**

Doctors

You can find a family doctor, also known as a general practitioner (GP), in every community. A GP helps look after people in their local area. These doctors also provide health education and carry out simple surgical operations. If a GP cannot deal with your problem, you will usually be referred to a hospital. You and your family must register with a GP to receive care.

GPs usually work in groups and their surgery provides a variety of services including care from nurses, health visitors and midwives.

 **Web help**

Find a doctor

www.nhs.uk/Service-Search/GP/LocationSearch/4

Registering with a GP surgery

Once you have chosen a doctor's surgery you should contact them and ask to register. They will usually ask you to complete a form, giving details such as:

- your name and address
- your date of birth
- your NHS number (if you know it)
- other information, such as the name and address of your previous GP
- your views on organ donation.

Sometimes they will ask to see proof of your identity. You may be asked to show:

- photo identity, such as your passport or driving licence
- proof of your address, such as a recent utility bill or council tax bill.

The GP surgery will send your form to your local NHS Commissioning Board area team. Your medical records will then be transferred to the new surgery.

If you are visiting an area for more than 24 hours but less than three months, you can apply to register with a GP surgery as a temporary resident. If you stay longer, you will have to re-register or become a permanent patient.

A surgery may ask you for your NHS medical card or your NHS number. This is helpful but it is not necessary to have it to register with a GP or to get NHS treatment.

Once registered, you'll be invited to make an appointment for a health check in the next six months. The practice nurse will usually carry out the check and will ask you about your personal and family medical history. They will also make sure that any tests or checks you need are up to date, such as measuring your blood pressure or arranging cervical screening.

 Action

Find out where your nearest GP is located.

Hospitals

NHS hospital treatment is free only to people who are ordinarily resident in the UK or are exempt from charges. Some specific services are free to everyone. These include:

- treatment for most infectious diseases (but not HIV treatment, apart from testing and counselling)
- treatment given inside an Accident and Emergency (A & E) department (but not emergency treatment provided after admission to the hospital)

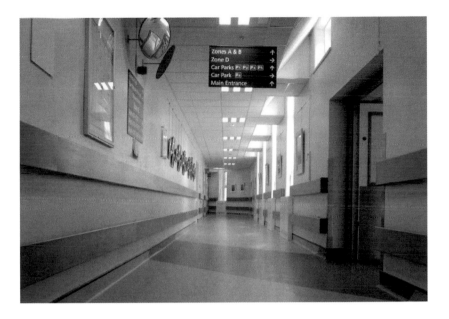

- compulsory psychiatric treatment
- compulsory treatment ordered by a court
- family planning services.

Dentists

Dentists may work for the NHS, offer private services or combine the two. It is a good idea to register with a dentist as soon as you move into a new area.

A dentist will examine you and then give you a written treatment plan if you need any work doing on your teeth. This lists all of the treatment that the dentist thinks you need. If you are with an NHS dentist there are extra charges for some treatments. You must agree to the plan before it can go ahead.

If you go to a private dentist, there are usually two ways of paying for treatment. Many people take out a 'dental payment plan' with a company. The type of policy you choose will depend on what you can afford to pay each month and what kind of treatment you think you might need. You can also be a 'private' patient and pay all your dental costs directly.

Opticians

There are opticians on every high street. They often offer a free eye test if you buy glasses or contact lenses from them. You may get help with payment from your employer or the state. Some people may receive help with paying for glasses. You will need to ask your optician whether you are eligible.

What if there is an emergency?

There are two emergency phone numbers you can use in the UK. The one most people know is 999. You can also use 112, which is the emergency number for all the countries in the European Union (EU). Either of these numbers will take you through to the police, fire brigade and ambulance service. Keep calm and answer the questions you are asked. The person on the phone will be trying to find out how best to help you.

There are other numbers which you can call when you want information but you are not in a crisis situation.

You can call 101 to report a crime that has already happened or to ask for advice on crime prevention. You can also report on any policing issues in your local area.

You can call 111 when you have a health problem that does not require the urgent response of a 999 call. It is available 24 hours a day and calls are free from landlines and mobile phones. You should use this number if you:

- need medical help fast but it's not a 999 emergency
- think you need to go to A&E or need another NHS urgent care service
- don't know who to call or you don't have a GP
- you need health information or reassurance about what to do next.

? **Web help**

Other support services

www.nhs.uk/symptomcheckers/Pages/UsefulPhoneNumbers.aspx

Registering a birth

A child born in the UK must have a birth certificate. To get one, you must go to the register office near where you live. In England, Wales and Northern Ireland you must register your baby within 42 days of the birth. In Scotland you need to do this within 21 days. The birth certificate is a very important document. Your child will need it throughout their life.

A mother can always register her child's birth on her own. A father can only do this if he was married to the mother when the baby was conceived or if the form is completed by both parents.

⬚! Action

Find out how you can get urgent treatment near where you live.

Find the location of your nearest register office.

Education

State education in the UK is free and all children between the ages of 5 and 16 must get an appropriate education. In Northern Ireland children start school at the age of 4. From 2015, all children in England born on or after 1 September 1997 must be either in education or receiving some form of training until they are 18. If you do not ensure your children are educated, you can be prosecuted and sent to prison. You are responsible for getting them to school on time every day of each term.

Most schools have uniforms and provide school meals. If you are on a low income you can get help with these costs. You may also have to pay for things such as school trips and music lessons. Sometimes a school is able to help with the cost of trips.

If your children speak very little English, a specialist teacher will support them at school.

Education from babyhood to adult life

Schools

Applying for a school place

First, you should go and visit schools nearby to choose the one that you think would be best for your child. Once you have decided, you fill in an application form. You will probably be asked to list schools in order of preference because your child may not get a place in the school of your choice. The application system varies across the UK.

- **England and Wales:** You apply for a place at most schools through the local council. Some schools have entrance exams and you have to apply directly. To find out more about the process in your area, contact your local authority.

- **Scotland:** Schools are in 'catchment areas' so most people go to their nearest primary or secondary school. You can request a place at a school outside your catchment area, but usually you will only get a place if there are spaces. You register for a school place through the local education authority.

- **Northern Ireland:** You apply to the Education and Library Boards for a school place. Some secondary schools have entrance exams, but the exam results can only be used to allocate places if the school is over-subscribed.

There are many independent schools for children of all ages in the UK. Some are boarding schools and others are day schools. Some offer both day and boarding places. Such schools are not dependent on the government for financing what they do, and are run by independent boards. They all charge fees.

? **Web help**

Applying for school places

For more information about applying for school places in different parts of the UK:

In England and Wales:
www.gov.uk/apply-for-primary-school-place
www.gov.uk/apply-for-secondary-school-place

In Scotland: **www.ltscotland.org.uk**

In Northern Ireland: **www.deni.gov.uk**

! **Action**

How do you get help with paying for the extras involved in educating children?

Find out how you apply for a school place where you live.

Types of school

There are a variety of schools in the UK. The pattern is fairly standard for children under 11. After this age, there are several different types of schools for children to attend.

- **Nursery schools** are available if parents want to send their children to school from the age of 3 to 5.

- **Primary schools** are often close to home and children stay with the same teacher all day. Most children from age 5 to 11 go to a primary school. Some regions have what are called first and middle schools, or infant and junior schools, and the age ranges may be different. Parents are expected to help young children with reading at home.

- **Free schools** can be found across the country. They may be primary or secondary and are set up by independent groups.

- **Academies** are publicly funded independent schools that used to be under the control of the local education authority. They get money direct from the government. Academies can take all ages of children. Some academies have sponsors such as businesses, universities, other schools, faith groups or voluntary groups. Sponsors are responsible for improving the performance of their schools.

- **Secondary or high schools** are larger than primary schools and children are taught each subject by a different teacher. Most secondary schools are for children from ages 11 to 16 (or 18 if there is a 'sixth form'). Again, there may be differences between regions of the country. Children are expected to complete independent work ('homework') outside of lessons.

- **Faith schools** are often linked to the Church of England or the Roman Catholic Church. There are also Muslim, Jewish and Sikh schools in some areas. Integrated schools in Northern Ireland aim to bring different Christian denominations together.

- **Independent schools** are private schools and parents have to pay fees. They are sometimes called 'public' schools.

- **Home schooling** is an option for parents who want to educate their children themselves. You will have to prove that you are doing it properly. There is no state funding.

The school curriculum
Each of the four countries of the UK plans its own curriculum which describes the topics that are taught in school. They have much in common but there are regional differences. Welsh, for example, is

taught in Wales. England, Wales and Northern Ireland take exams known as the General Certificate of Secondary Education (GCSE) at age 16 and A-levels at 18. In Scotland there are Standard Grade exams and Highers for the same age groups.

Independent schools do not have to follow the curriculum in any area of the UK. Certain types of state-funded school in England also do not have to follow the national curriculum.

Assessment: 4 to 16

The curriculum in primary schools in England, Wales and Northern Ireland is divided into two key stages and children's progress is monitored against the standards that are expected. This assessment is carried out by their teachers and reported to their parents.

At age 11 children sit Standard Assessment Tests, commonly known as SATs. In some areas there are selective secondary schools and children have to sit an exam to go to one of these schools.

In secondary schools, most students sit GCSE exams at age 16. These cover a wide range of curriculum areas. There are also other exams available to meet the needs of students. In Scotland the pattern is similar but the exams are called Standard Grade.

? Web help

The school curriculum

You can find out more about the different curricula in the UK at the following websites:

England: **www.gov.uk/national-curriculum**

Wales: **http://wales.gov.uk/topics/educationandskills/ schoolshome**

Scotland: **www.educationscotland.gov.uk/thecurriculum**

Northern Ireland: **www.nicurriculum.org.uk**

The education system in different parts of the UK

England and Wales

Nursery education is free but not compulsory. From the age of 3, children in England have the right to 15 hours a week of free nursery education for 38 weeks of the year. In Wales it is 10 hours a week from the age of 3.

Children in England and Wales generally start school in the September after their fourth birthday. Parents can choose to keep their children at home for longer but they must start school from the beginning of the term after their fifth birthday. Some schools in Wales teach mainly in Welsh.

Most children in England go to a primary school between the ages of 5 and 11 and then move to a secondary school. Some schools have a sixth form so students stay until they are 18. In many areas there are sixth form colleges which students attend from age 16 to 18.

Some areas of England have middle schools which cater for students from age 8 or 9 to age 12 or 13.

The table shows the structure of schools and the curriculum in England and Wales.

School structure in England and Wales

Age on 31 August	Year group	Curriculum stage	Type of school		
3	Nursery	Foundation	Nursery		
4	Reception		Primary school	Infant school	First school
5	1	Key stage 1			
6	2				
7	3	Key stage 2		Junior school	
8	4				
9	5				
10	6				Middle school
11	7	Key stage 3	Secondary school*		
12	8				
13	9				Upper school
14	10	Key stage 4			
15	11				
16	12	Sixth form			
17	13				

Scotland

As soon as children become 3 years old they are can have up to 475 hours of nursery education a year until they start primary school. This is free and optional.

If your child's fifth birthday is between the beginning of March and the end of the following February they can start school in the August of that year. You can choose a later start date in that period if you wish.

Most children go to primary school for seven years and high school for four to six years. Some schools in rural areas have schools for students from Primary 1 to S4 or S6.

School structure in Scotland

Age at start of school year (August)	Year group	Type of school
4–5	Primary 1	Primary school
5–6	Primary 2	
6–7	Primary 3	
7–8	Primary 4	
8–9	Primary 5	
9–10	Primary 6	
10–11	Primary 7	
11–12	S1	High school
12–13	S2	
13–14	S3	
14–15	S4	
15–16	S5	
16–17	S6	

School structure in Northern Ireland

Age on 1 July	Year group	Curriculum stage	Type of school
4	Primary 1	Foundation	Primary school
5	Primary 2		
6	Primary 3	Key stage 1	
7	Primary 4		
8	Primary 5	Key stage 2	
9	Primary 6		
10	Primary 7		
11	8	Key stage 3	Secondary school
12	9		
13	10		
14	11	Key stage 4	
15	12		
16	13	Sixth form	
17	14		

Northern Ireland

In Northern Ireland, nursery education is optional. There are free places available but priority is given to children from disadvantaged backgrounds. Children generally go to nursery for two and a half hours a day. Some nurseries offer four hours.

If your child turns 4 on or before 1 July they will start school in September.

Children attend a primary school and then a secondary school. Some secondary schools do not have a sixth form and students go to a separate sixth form college.

 Action

Look up the Ofsted reports for schools in your area.

If you have children, which school do you think would suit them best?

Choices at 16

Improve exam grades

Stay at school

Take a vocational course for a specific career

Go to a further education college

Take an academic course for higher education and some careers

Get a job and have work-based training

At 16, teenagers must consider their options.

School leaving age

In England, all students must stay in education until they are 17 years old. They don't have to stay at school but they must take one of these three options:

- Stay in full-time education at school or college.
- Start an apprenticeship.
- Take a job, be self-employed or become a volunteer and be in part-time education or training.

In Wales, Scotland and Northern Ireland students can leave school at 16.

Making career choices

Students in schools and colleges receive careers education when they have choices to make about their future pathways through education. At the age of 13 (in Year 9) they will be selecting GCSEs or other courses. Between 16 and 18, they will be making decisions about higher education and employment.

[?] **Web help**

Career planning

The National Careers Service website offers a wide range of advice on careers: **https://nationalcareersservice.direct.gov.uk/Pages/Home.aspx**

The post-16 curriculum

Young people who stay at school or go to a college of further education (FE) can take a range of qualifications, depending on their future plans. Those who want to go to university generally take A-levels (or Highers in Scotland). Other qualifications can lead to university. If a student knows what job they want to get then there may be special courses they can take. Some students, who have not got the GCSE grades they want, may go to college to improve on them. They can then progress to their chosen career.

 Web help

Funding education from ages 16 to 18

Funding for this age group no longer operates in England, but you can find out about support in Scotland, Wales and Northern Ireland: **www.gov.uk/education-maintenance-allowance-ema**

The role of parents

As a parent, you may be asked to sign a home-school agreement, which sets out what you are expected to do to support your child's education. This will cover things such as ensuring that homework is done, buying the correct uniform and making sure your child wears it. Parents often go into schools to help in the classroom in a variety of ways. You can also become a school governor or member of the school board. This is an important role as it is responsible for the wellbeing of the school as a whole. Most schools have a parents' association which raises funds and organises social events for parents.

You will receive reports and the chance to have meetings with the teachers to discuss your child's work and progress. Many schools send out a newsletter every week to tell you what is going on. This is now often sent to an email address to make sure parents get the news.

As a parent you must make sure your children attend school. If a child is ill, you must contact the school and explain the absence straight away. You are not allowed to take children on holiday during term time - you may be fined if you do so.

Going to university

Many people go to university at the age of 18. In England, Wales and Northern Ireland most students have to pay tuition fees. The amount depends on where in the UK they are from and where they study.

Students from Scotland do not pay fees if they study in Scotland or another EU country. Students from England, Wales and Northern Ireland do have to pay fees in Scotland. Some students can get help with paying their fees through bursaries from the government or university.

Most students get a low-interest student loan to help pay their living expenses when they are at university. They start paying it back when they are working and earn above a certain amount. Your eligibility for a student loan may depend on your immigration status.

Budgeting

Learning to manage money so that there is a balance between having enough cash to pay for essentials (such as food and rent) and enjoying a social life is all part of the university experience.

Most banks offer student accounts which give useful benefits such as cheap or free overdrafts, providing you don't go over your limit.

? Web help

Applying to university

www.gov.uk/higher-education-courses-find-and-apply

www.gov.uk/student-finance-calculator

For information on university funding

Wales: **www.studentfinancewales.co.uk**

Scotland: **www.saas.gov.uk**

Northern Ireland: **www.studentfinanceni.co.uk**

Find out about budgeting: **www.ucas.com/how-it-all-works/ student-finance/managing-money/figuring-out-budget**

Adult education

Some colleges offer courses to adults over the age of 18 including:

- English for speakers of other languages
- literacy and numeracy
- skills for employment.

There are also classes for those who just want to study, meet other people and develop a skill or hobby. There are fees for these courses.

! Action

Find out about classes for adults at your local college. Your local authority website will probably offer help.

Chapter 5

Community life

In this chapter your will learn about:

- Local government
- Culture, heritage and sport
- Your community

Local government

Councils

In the UK we vote for councillors to run local government. Every area across the country elects a councillor to parish or town councils, district councils and county councils. Being a councillor carries a great deal of responsibility, but the role is usually voluntary. Councillors are paid travel expenses and an attendance fee for meetings, but they don't usually receive a salary. As a UK citizen, you can stand for election to your local council.

When the district or county council meets after an election, it elects a leader and the members of the cabinet, if there is one. These councillors come from the political party that won a majority in the election. Each member of the cabinet is responsible for one area of the council's work, such as education, social services, finance, and leisure and recreation.

The area that a councillor represents is known as a ward. When they vote, councillors must represent all the people in their ward.

Most councillors have full-time jobs so they cannot run all the council services as well. A chief executive is appointed to take responsibility for this. In each department, people who are experts in their field are employed to make sure it all runs smoothly.

In some places, the leader of the council is known as the mayor. A mayor often has little power but takes part in local ceremonies and greets important people when they come on formal visits.

A number of places, including London, have elected mayors who have a lot more power. The Mayor of London, for example, sets an overall vision for London and has a duty to create plans and policies for the capital covering:

- transport
- planning and development
- housing
- economic development and regeneration
- culture
- health inequalities
- environmental issues including climate change, waste disposal and air quality.

The mayor has a number of other duties relating to culture and tourism, including managing Trafalgar Square and Parliament Square.

What does the council do?

Your local council is responsible for a range of services for your community.

Local councils are responsible for community services

The council sets the budget for each area of spending. The amount of money spent will depend on many different things. Here are some examples:

- In an area where the population is very young, they will need lots of schools.
- Where there are many old people, they may need help from social services.
- If there are lots of people, there will be lots of refuse to collect.

As the amount of money a council can spend is limited by central government it must work out its priorities. There is never enough money to provide everything, so when you vote in local elections you are helping the council to decide what its priorities will be.

The money to pay for local services comes from a mix of sources. Much of it comes from central government and the rest is funded from the local area.

- **Council tax** is paid by all the adults living in the area. The amount each person pays depends on the value of the house they live in. If you live in a big house you pay more than people who live in smaller houses.
- **Business rates** are paid by local businesses. The amount depends on the rent that could be charged for the office, shop or factory that the business uses. The business rate is collected by central government and redistributed across the country.

The amount of money that central government pays depends on the needs of each area and how much can be raised locally.

Everything a council does is discussed at council meetings. These are open to the public and there is always time on the agenda for local people to have their say.

 Web help

Your local council

Use the internet to find the website of your local council.

Find out how much you pay in the different bands of council tax.

Are there any services provided by the council that you didn't know about?

! **Action**

Who is your local councillor? Do they represent a political party?

Which services do you use that are provided by the local council?

Culture, heritage and sport

Religion

In the UK you are free to practise your own religion. You will find different religious groups in most towns and cities across the country. The UK has historically been a mainly Christian country, and Christianity is still the largest religion.

The official state church in England is the Church of England (also known as the Anglican Church), with the monarch as its head.

The Archbishop of Canterbury is the leader of the Church of England. A church committee recommends a candidate for this position to the Prime Minister who submits the name to the Queen for approval.

The national church of Scotland is the Presbyterian Church. It is led by the Moderator and the General Assembly of the Church of Scotland. Northern Ireland and Wales do not have established churches.

There are several Protestant Christian groups in the UK apart from the Church of England. These include Quakers, Presbyterians, the Methodist Church, the United Reformed Church and the Baptist

Church. The Roman Catholic Church is the largest Christian denomination in the UK after the Church of England.

Islam, Hinduism, Judaism, Sikhism and Buddhism are all to be found in the UK.

An internet search will help you find your nearest place of worship.

Customs and festivals

In the UK we have a range of festival days and events. Some are holidays – but not all.

The Christian year

Christmas

On 25 December, people in the UK celebrate Christmas, which represents the birth of Jesus Christ.

Both 25 and 26 December are public holidays and are a time for festivities for both people who have religious beliefs and those who don't.

On Christmas Eve (24 December), children hang up their stockings, hoping for presents from 'Father Christmas'. They usually find them filled up when they wake in the morning. They may have left a glass of sherry and a mince pie out for Father Christmas when he arrives. Before they go to bed, Mummy and Daddy will have eaten and drunk them, leaving only a few crumbs – just to prove that Father Christmas really came in the night!

Presents are exchanged on Christmas Day

On Christmas Day, families try to get together, exchange presents and have special meals. The traditional meal is turkey, Christmas pudding and mince pies – though people often cook their own variations, too.

Church services are held at midnight on Christmas Eve and on Christmas morning. The congregation sings traditional carols. In the weeks before Christmas you may also hear carols sung by people knocking on your door as they raise money for good causes.

Easter

Easter is the most sacred day in the Christian calendar. According to the Bible, Jesus died on Good Friday and rose again on Easter Day. Easter Monday is a public holiday.

The six-week period leading up to Easter is called Lent, and Christians often give up something they enjoy during this time. The day before Lent begins is called Shrove Tuesday and is a day when many British people eat pancakes. There are often events at schools, such as pancake races where children have to run while trying to toss a pancake.

Many people celebrate Easter with chocolate Easter eggs and people often organise Easter egg hunts for children. They represent the coming of spring.

Easter changes date from year to year. It is in either March or April.

Festivals of other religions

As the UK is a diverse society we recognise the special days of other religions.

Eid al-Fitr takes place at the end of Ramadan, when Muslims have fasted for a month. Muslims attend special services and meals and thank Allah for giving them the strength to complete the fast. The date when it takes places changes every year. There are often celebrations in areas with large Muslim communities. In the centre of London, for instance, it is a big event with food, music and theatre. People may be given a day off work although it is not a public holiday.

Eid ul Adha reminds Muslims of their commitment to God as they reflect on the act of the prophet Ibrahim who was willing to sacrifice his son when God ordered him to. Many Muslims sacrifice an animal to eat during this festival. In the UK this has to be done in a slaughterhouse.

Diwali is celebrated by Hindus and Sikhs. It last for five days in October or November. It celebrates the victory of good over evil and is often called the 'Festival of Lights'. There are different stories about how it came about. Leicester hosts a famous celebration as there is a strong community in the town. A whole week of festivities is organised, including special street lighting, music, dancing, exhibitions and traditional food. All the big cities stage firework displays to mark the event.

Hannukah is a time when Jews remember their struggle for religious freedom. It takes place in November or December and lasts for eight days. On each day of the festival a candle is lit on a stand of eight (menorah) to remember the story of the festival, where oil that should have lasted only a day did so for eight. It is also known as the 'Festival of Lights'.

Patron saints' days

The four countries of the UK all have patron saints. In Scotland and Northern Ireland, patron saint days are public holidays. There are some celebrations in England and Wales on St George's Day and St David's Day respectively.

- 1 March: St David's Day, Wales
- 17 March: St Patrick's Day, Northern Ireland
- 23 April: St George's Day, England
- 30 November: St Andrew's Day, Scotland

Non-religious festivals and celebrations

31 December to 1 January – New Year's Eve to New Year's Day
The arrival of the new year is celebrated from the evening of 31 December, when people often go to parties or visit friends. As the clock chimes midnight, people often sing *Auld Lang Syne*, a traditional New Year's song originally from Scotland that has gradually spread over the British Isles.

In Scotland, the celebration is called Hogmanay (which is the word in Scots meaning the last day of the year). Hogmanay is the traditional celebration at this time of year in Scotland and can be a bigger event than Christmas. In major Scottish cities the parties continue through the night. In the rest of the UK only 1 January is a public holiday but in Scotland they have 2 January as well.

25 January – Burns Night

Robert Burns was a Scottish poet, most famous for writing *Auld Lang Syne*. Burns Night celebrates his birthday on 25 January. People sit down to a meal of haggis (a special type of sausage) and 'tatties and neeps' – potatoes and turnips (but these turnips are called swedes in England). They make a toast to the haggis with glasses of whisky. Burns Night also involves bagpipes (a Scottish musical instrument) and readings of Burns' poetry.

Late January to mid-February – Chinese New Year

Chinese New Year is a great festival for Chinese communities in London and across the world. It is based on the lunar and solar calendars. Each year in the Chinese calendar is represented by one of the 12 animals of the Chinese zodiac. The date of Chinese New Year varies, but always takes place between late January and mid-February.

The festivities in central London take place in Trafalgar Square, Chinatown and Shaftesbury Avenue. There is a lively parade and visiting artists from China perform on the main stage in Trafalgar Square. You will find Lion teams, performances from local artists and traditional food and craft stalls.

14 February – Valentine's Day

People in love exchange cards and gifts. Sometimes anonymous cards are sent from secret admirers – which can lead to confusion!

1 April – April Fool's Day

People play jokes on each other before midday. There are often April Fools' jokes in the form of invented stories in the newspapers and on the radio. People have to listen carefully so they are not caught out.

Three weeks before Easter – Mothering Sunday
Mothers receive cards and presents from their children. They may be brought breakfast in bed.

Third Sunday in June – Father's Day
Fathers receive cards and presents from their children.

Mid-June – The Queen's Official Birthday
The Queen's birthday is officially celebrated by the ceremony of Trooping the Colour on a Saturday in June.

Although the Queen was born on 21 April, it has long been the tradition to celebrate the Sovereign's birthday publicly on a day in the summer, when good weather is more likely.

Trooping the Colour is carried out by soldiers of the Household Cavalry on horses as well as the Foot Guards. It takes place on Horse Guards Parade in Whitehall and is watched by members of the Royal Family, invited guests and members of the public.

21 June – Summer Solstice
The summer solstice is the longest day of the year and festivities are held across the country. Stonehenge, the historic monument in Wiltshire, is the main focus of celebrations. At least 20,000 people gather to celebrate the event. Druids, pagans and revellers join the all-night activities and wait for the sun to rise.

31 October – Halloween
An ancient festival which marks the beginning of winter. Faces are carved in pumpkins and young people often dress up in costumes to play 'trick or treat'. People stop them playing tricks by handing out 'treats' – usually sweets of some kind.

5 November – Bonfire Night
In 1605 a group of Catholics led by Guy Fawkes attempted and failed to kill the Protestant king (King James I) by bombing the Houses of Parliament. Today people light bonfires and set off fireworks at home or, more usually, at special displays. In many towns and cities, Bonfire Night is often celebrated on the Saturday closest to 5 November rather than on the actual date.

11 November – Remembrance Day
During the week or two before 11 November, people wear poppies in memory of those who died fighting in the First World War, Second World War and other wars. At 11.00 am on the 11th day of the 11th month, there is a two-minute silence.

Bank holidays
There are other bank holidays in early May (early May bank holiday), late May (spring bank holiday) and late August (summer bank holiday). In Northern Ireland, there is a bank holiday in mid-July (anniversary of the Battle of the Boyne), and Scotland has a bank holiday in late November/early December to celebrate St Andrew's Day. The dates change because they are always on a Monday – to give people a long weekend. Schools always close for bank holidays.

 **Web help**

Bank holidays

You can find out when bank holidays take place each year:
https://gov.uk/bank-holidays

Culture

Books and authors
The UK has produced many famous authors. Daniel Defoe was one of the earliest novelists. He is famous for *Robinson Crusoe*. His books popularised the novel as a style of literature in the 18th century.

The Brontë sisters were brought up in Haworth, Yorkshire during the 19th century. The three sisters, Charlotte, Emily and Anne were all authors and poets. At first they had to write under male names so that their work would be accepted. The sisters wrote *Jane Eyre, Wuthering Heights* and *The Tenant of Wildfell Hall*, all of which became known as masterpieces.

At about the same time, Charles Dickens, George Eliot and Anthony Trollope were writing books that told of life in the 19th century. George Eliot's real name was Mary Ann Evans – but like the Brontë sisters, she had to write under a man's name to be published. Sir Arthur Conan Doyle, a Scottish doctor, wrote stories about his famous fictional detective, Sherlock Holmes.

Sir Arthur Conan Doyle – author of the Sherlock Holmes books

Famous modern authors of fiction include Kingsley Amis (who wrote *Lucky Jim*) and his son, Martin. Martin Amis's books include *London Fields*. Other well-known writers are A.S. Byatt (*Possession*), J.K. Rowling (the *Harry Potter* books) and Terry Pratchett (the *Discworld* series). There is also a strong tradition of iconic writers from ethnic backgrounds, including Kazuo Ishiguro (*The Remains of the Day*) and Zadie Smith (*White Teeth*).

Poetry
The UK also has a reputation for the quality of its poetry. Seamus Heaney, from Northern Ireland, was a poet, playwright and translator. He won the Nobel Prize for Literature in 1995. Benjamin Zephaniah – a British-born poet of mixed Jamaican and Barbadian heritage – is famous for his public performances, and was listed in *The Times'* top-50 post-war authors.

Famous UK awards for literature

The Man Booker Prize for Fiction is awarded annually for the best fiction novel written in English and published In the UK. Winners include Ian McEwan, Hilary Mantel and Julian Barnes.

There are also various other prizes that recognise outstanding achievement in the field, such as the Somerset Maugham Award and the National Book Awards.

Theatre

Local communities across the country watch and take part in theatre productions. Semi-professional and professional performances are usually given in theatres with up-to-the-minute technology designed to create dramatic effects.

Everyone can take part – many towns and villages have amateur dramatic groups that regularly perform popular works. Many of these performances take place in village halls and community centres. During Christmas and New Year, pantomimes are often staged – these are musical comedies designed for families to enjoy. There are also some famous amateur groups which have their own theatres – or perform in pubs. The Tower Theatre Company, a very active group in central London, and the Maddermarket Theatre in Norwich are examples of such groups. For those people looking to study the theatre, there are also courses available in acting and production.

All the main cities and many smaller towns have theatres which put on professional plays. London's West End is considered the centre of the UK's theatrical tradition as there are many theatres in a small area. There is always a great variety of musicals, dance, opera and serious plays on at any time of the year.

Arts festivals

Arts festivals are held throughout the UK in many towns and cities. One of the most well-known is the Edinburgh Festival. There are hundreds of different arts and cultural events at the Festival and 'The Fringe' is particularly well known for its comedy and experimental theatre. Many young comedians have been spotted while performing at the Edinburgh Fringe.

Notting Hill Carnival is one of the most famous examples of a
European street carnival. Usually held over the August bank holiday,
it features Caribbean music, food and dancing from people of all
different backgrounds, as well as performances from established
international music acts. The carnival was originally established by
immigrants from the Caribbean.

Playwrights

William Shakespeare is the UK's most famous playwright and his
plays are often performed across the country and abroad. There are
many successful modern playwrights, including Alan Ayckbourn,
David Hare and Alan Bennett.

William Shakespeare

The Laurence Olivier Awards are named after one of Britain's famous Shakespearean actors. Awards are given to many categories of theatrical activity including best director, actor and actress.

Art galleries and museums

The UK has a wealth of art galleries and museums. The national art galleries in London, Cardiff and Edinburgh all have permanent collections of works by British and international artists. They often have special exhibitions on particular themes or specific artists.

Most major towns and cities have their own museums and art galleries, some of which have specialist themes relating to their local area. There are also museums that house collections about the different cultures that make up the UK, such as the Manchester Jewish Museum and the British Museum in London.

Famous British artists

In the early 19th century Joseph Turner painted many beautiful pictures of the land, and seascapes such as *The Fighting Téméraire*.

John Constable painted rural England at about the same time.

The Pre-Raphaelites were a group of artists who lived in the 19th century. They were founded by Holman Hunt who brought together others who would become famous, including Millais and Rossetti. Today their paintings are to be found in galleries across the country, with a particularly good collection in Birmingham City Art Gallery.

David Hockney is one of the UK's most famous contemporary painters. He has recently expanded his work by creating beautiful works using his iPad.

The Tate is the UK's most famous group of galleries. Tate Britain focuses on British Art. Tate Modern has a collection of 20th and 21st century art. There are also Tate Galleries in St Ives in Cornwall and Liverpool.

The Turner Prize, named after the artist, was set up in 1984 and celebrates contemporary art. The winner is selected from four works which have been shortlisted and shown at Tate Britain.

It is one of the most prestigious art awards in Europe. In the past Damien Hirst, Sir Anish Kapoor, Rachel Whiteread and Richard Wright have been winners.

? Web help

Galleries

Most galleries have websites which tell you about their permanent collections and current exhibitions. Here are five, but you can find many more online.

Nation Gallery London: **www.nationalgallery.org.uk**

National Museum Cardiff: **www.museumwales.ac.uk**

National Galleries Edinburgh: **www.nationalgalleries.org**

Birmingham Museum and Art Gallery: **www.bmag.org.uk**

Tate Galleries: **www.tate.org.uk**

Music

Music plays an important part in British life. The country has a long history of composing and performing music as diverse as orchestral pieces, pop songs and show music.

During the summer, the Proms can be heard in various venues in London, including on a big screen in Hyde Park and on the radio. The Last Night of the Proms is also televised. A wide range of classical music from the UK and around the world is performed.

Music events of all kinds are performed at very large venues such as Wembley Stadium and The O2 Arena (both in London), and the Scottish Exhibition and Conference Centre (SECC) in Glasgow.

Glastonbury festival

Glastonbury is the most famous summer festival in the UK. It is one of many that are held all over the country. People take their tents and stay for several days to enjoy the music of famous and up-and-coming bands and solo performers. Other smaller festivals celebrate different kinds of music, ranging from jazz, rock and pop, to folk and classical.

Getting involved with music

Some pubs and clubs have 'open mic' nights that give unknown musicians the opportunity to perform in front of a live audience. Check the internet for information about open mic nights in your area.

Sport

People from all over the world follow the fortunes of the football clubs in the English Premiership. There is, however, much more to sport in the UK than this.

All sorts of sport are played at all levels – from fully professional teams to amateurs playing in the local park. There are clubs and classes for almost everything you can think of – from individual sports such as martial arts and tennis, to team games such as hockey and basketball.

Playing sport is good for your health and an excellent way of making friends. If you want to find out more about what is available, your local leisure centre is a good place to start. You could also carry out an internet search as many sports clubs have websites.

Your local council may also have an active website to help you find out what sporting activities are going on near you. Some local councils run sports classes, for which there is usually a fee. They may also arrange sporting activities for children after school and during the holidays. Swimming lessons are particularly important for children so that they can be safe near water.

Private sports clubs and fitness centres run classes too. There is usually a fee to join and an annual subscription, as well as an additional fee for the classes.

？ Web help

Find out more about the sports activities in your area by visiting these websites. If your favourite sport isn't on the list, try searching the internet for more information.

Cricket: **www.ecb.co.uk/development**

Football: **www.thefa.com/my-football**

Rugby League: **www.therfl.co.uk/more/play**

Rugby Union: **www.rfu.com/takingpart**

Tennis: **http://www.lta.org.uk/players-parents**

You and your community

Living in the UK involves being part of a community. You may be part of a big city or a small village. Wherever it is, they all have one thing in common. You will be surrounded by other people and have the opportunity to join this community.

What is your role in the community?

People in the UK believe that there is a set of values which everyone should share. This is particularly important because the UK's society is very diverse and common values draw people together. If you take on these values and responsibilities, you will find it much easier to be part of your community.

Behave morally and ethically

Look after the environment

Obey the law

Have respect for everyone regardless of sex, race, religion, age, disability, class or sexual orientation

Vote in elections if you are entitled to do so

Be fair to others and respect them

Be responsible for your actions

Support and provide for your family

Help other people

Your values and responsibilities

Getting to know your neighbours

The people who live near you can help you to settle into a new community so it is important to introduce yourself to them. They probably have lots of information about how things work and where you can find local services. They will probably know all about local schools, doctors and dentists.

You may be able to help them – for example, by putting out the wheelie bins if they are away or feeding their cat or dog if necessary. If you do things like this, your neighbours are likely to help you when you need support.

Sometimes neighbours have disagreements. It is wise to avoid such problems if you can. People get upset when neighbours make too much noise, particularly late at night. If all the gardens are tidy, it's important that yours is too or people will think you are letting the neighbourhood down.

Community centres

Many towns and cities have ethnic community centres. These often provide advice and support to newly arrived immigrants and can be an excellent source of information for people wanting to get to know people in their local community. Some may offer educational opportunities as well as encourage participation in community life between people of different ethnic backgrounds.

Libraries

Most towns and cities – and some larger villages – have a library. Libraries usually allow you to borrow books, free of charge, for an agreed time limit before you have to take them back. Some also offer CDs and DVDs – though borrowing these may mean you have to pay a small charge. You can also find out about more about what is going on in your local area and get useful information about how to access local services.

In rural areas there are sometimes mobile libraries. These are large vans, filled with shelves of books, that travel between villages. They make it easier for people who find it difficult to travel to their nearest library.

> **! Action**
>
> **Use the internet to search for community centres in your area. Councils' websites often have links to useful resources and you may be able to get more information from your local library.**
>
> **Look on the internet for your local library and make a note of what services it provides.**

Joining local activities

Wherever you live, there are organisations which can use your help. You may have the skill to do something that is very useful to local organisations – whether it is cooking food for community events or dealing with their administrative needs. By joining in, you are showing people that you hold the same values as theirs. Your contribution will help to make your community a better place.

Volunteering

Volunteering means working for good causes without payment. Not only does this help the good cause but it also helps the volunteer. Many people offer their services because they enjoy helping other people but there is also a practical side to volunteering.

It helps you to:

- meet people in your community
- learn new skills
- develop skills which may help you get a job
- improve your English.

There are many opportunities to volunteer. Community Service Volunteers is a volunteering and social action charity that helps people to get involved in their local communities. If you have some free time and want to contribute to a cause that you care about, then search the internet for opportunities to help in your area.

? Web help

Want to volunteer?

www.csv.org.uk

www.do-it.org.uk

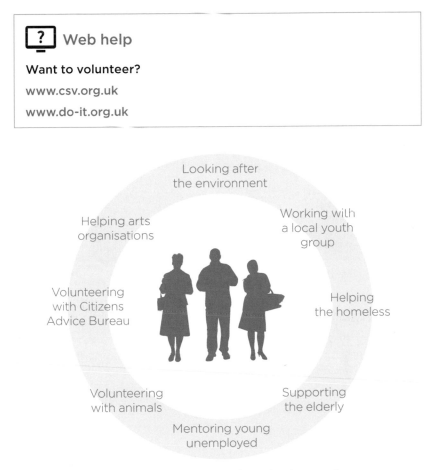

Some of the many ways you can get involved with your local community

There are many charities looking for your help. Some have charity shops all over the country which are staffed by volunteers. Look at your high street and see if there is one which serves a good cause you would like to support. For example, Age UK supports the elderly, Oxfam combats international poverty and the People's Dispensary for Sick Animals (PDSA) looks after animals. There are many others which support local hospices, children's charities and other local causes.

Charity shops selling donated clothes rely on volunteers

If you are interested in the UK's heritage you might want to volunteer with the National Trust. It is the biggest landowner in the UK and looks after a wide variety of places, such as stretches of coastline, moorland and farms. It also owns historic buildings, including 'stately homes', and gardens. Volunteers help to keep National Trust properties open by staffing them and helping with their upkeep.

Some organisations specialise in encouraging young people to volunteer. They aim to help them to develop their skills and some offer qualifications relating to these activities. Volunteering can therefore improve your CV and help you to gain places for higher education or employment.

? Web help

Young volunteers

England: **www.vinspired.com**

Wales: **www.gwirvol.org**

Scotland: **www.vds.org.uk**

Northern Ireland: **www.volunteernow.co.uk**

How can you support your community?

In schools

Schools often welcome volunteers who support their activities. Whether you have children or not, your skills and expertise can be put to good use. There are many ways in which you can help. Listening to children read means they get more individual attention and time to practise. You might talk to groups about your experiences in other parts of the world or just offer help with general activities regularly. Depending on your role, you may need to be checked by the Disclosure and Barring Service (DBS) to make sure you have no record that would exclude you from such activities.

If you are a parent, you will know all about the school's activities from information sent home with your children. There are often fund raising activities to buy extra equipment for the school. These include Christmas fairs and summer fêtes, which may need people to help staff the stalls and bring products to sell. Perhaps you could make some interesting food for such events or social evenings when parents get together in informal ways.

Most schools have parent/teacher associations which organise events. Offers of help with the administration are always welcome and will help you to get to know your local community.

Being a school governor, or a member of a school board in Scotland, is a more formal way of helping in school. It involves playing a key part in the development of the school. You would be responsible, with others, for:

- setting the strategic direction of the school
- ensuring accountability
- monitoring and evaluating school performance.

Governors and board members are elected or appointed, usually for a period of four years. They aim to improve the quality of education and standards of achievement at the school. They are involved with development planning, policy making, monitoring and evaluating performance, setting targets for pupil performance and making sure that people are acting responsibly.

Governors regularly visit the school to listen to reading, work in the library, assist with school trips and support staff in the classroom.

? **Web help**

School governors and board members

To find out more:

In England: **www.gov.uk/become-school-college-governor**

In Wales: **www.governorswales.org.uk**

In Scotland:
www.scotland.gov.uk/Publications/2004/09/19902/42690

In Northern Ireland:
www.nidirect.gov.uk/becoming-a-school-governor

Blood and organ donation

Hospitals in the UK need blood to help people survive operations and illnesses. It is freely donated by members of the public. The donor service sets up events in the local area for people to give blood. It does not take very long and provides a service which helps people in serious need.

There are many people in need of an organ transplant. It is a very difficult decision for your relatives to make if you die suddenly, so you can make it much easier if you are already registered as a donor.

 **Web help**

Blood donors and organ donation

You can find out more about the process:

England and North Wales: **www.blood.co.uk**

Rest of Wales: **www.welsh-blood.org.uk**

Scotland: **www.scotblood.co.uk**

Northern Ireland: **www.nibts.org**

For organ donation: **www.organdonation.nhs.uk**

Jury service

In Crown Courts in England and Wales, Sheriff Courts and the High Court in Scotland, juries decide whether people are innocent or guilty. They hear the more serious criminal cases such as theft, burglary, murder and drugs offences. If a defendant is found guilty, the judge will decide on the penalty.

Once you are on the electoral register, you may be chosen at random to serve on a jury.

Being a juror is a very important role and a chance to do something positive for the community. You may be allowed to defer your jury service once but you are expected to accept on a second occasion.

Web help

Jury service

To find out more: **www.gov.uk/jury-service**

Joining a political party

Political parties are always looking for members and volunteers to help them promote their causes. At election time, they need people to support their local candidate by canvassing. This means knocking on doors to ask whether the residents will support their candidate. You may also be asked to deliver leaflets in residential areas.

Looking after the environment

There is much concern about damage to the environment, so it is important that we all do what we can to prevent the situation getting worse. Most parts of the UK arrange refuse collections to help reduce and recycle the amount of waste we produce. Card, plastic bottles and glass are mostly recyclable. You will be provided with bins and boxes which will be collected regularly. It is important to do this so we don't have to use more resources than is necessary and put as little as possible into landfill.

You can take all sorts of things to your local recycling centre where they will be dealt with in the best way possible. Larger centres can take old paint, broken electrical goods such as kettles and metal. Sometimes you can also take furniture or other items such as books that will then be offered to charities and people in need.

Freecycle is an organisation which helps people to give things away rather than throwing them away. You can find details of your local Freecycle group on the internet.

You can also help by shopping in your local community and buying products which are produced locally. This will reduce your 'carbon footprint' because the product has not been transported a long distance and you do not have to travel far to buy it. Many of the fruit and vegetables eaten in the UK are flown in by plane and therefore use up more carbon, which increases global warming.

Walking and using public transport also helps because it produces less pollution than everyone using their cars.

[?] **Web help**

The environment

Find out how you can help look after the environment:

www.recyclenow.com

www.wasteawarenesswales.org.uk

www.recycleforscotland.com

https://www.freecycle.org

Chapter 6

Out and about

In this chapter you will learn about:

- Places of interest
- Traditions
- Transport
- Leisure

The UK: geography and heritage

The UK's landscape is very varied for such a small country. There are dramatic coastlines as well as areas of gentle, rolling countryside. There are also major world cities with many famous buildings that reflect the long history of the UK.

You can see some famous landmarks on the accompanying map.

The UK's landscape

The UK presents a rich and diverse landscape. You can wander through the countryside and along coastal paths in any part of the country. Even in big cities, the countryside is not far away.

There are many public footpaths, which are shown on Ordnance Survey maps. These maps cover the whole country and can be bought in bookshops or on the internet. They also provide you with pointers to interesting places, national trails such as the Ridgeway or the South West Coastal Path and the national parks.

The following pictures show some major places of interest from around the UK. You may have seen them before in tourist guides or on the television. Remember that if you plan to visit any of these places, they are likely to be busier on public holidays and at weekends.

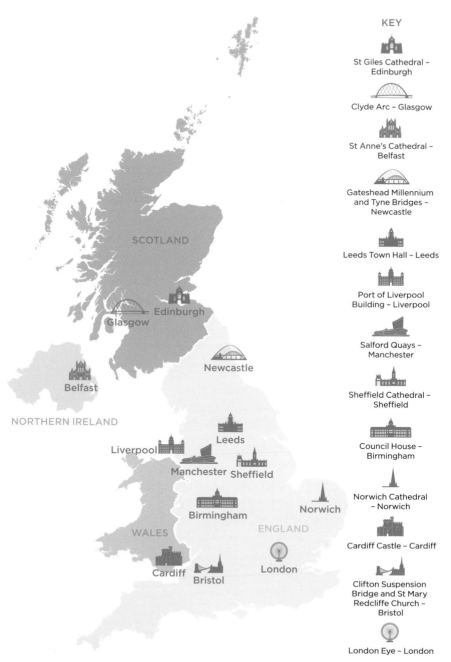

KEY

St Giles Cathedral – Edinburgh

Clyde Arc – Glasgow

St Anne's Cathedral – Belfast

Gateshead Millennium and Tyne Bridges – Newcastle

Leeds Town Hall – Leeds

Port of Liverpool Building – Liverpool

Salford Quays – Manchester

Sheffield Cathedral – Sheffield

Council House – Birmingham

Norwich Cathedral – Norwich

Cardiff Castle – Cardiff

Clifton Suspension Bridge and St Mary Redcliffe Church – Bristol

London Eye – London

SCOTLAND

Glasgow

Edinburgh

Newcastle

Belfast

NORTHERN IRELAND

Liverpool

Leeds

Manchester

Sheffield

Birmingham

Norwich

WALES

ENGLAND

Cardiff

Bristol

London

Some major landmarks of the UK

Tower Bridge stretches over the River Thames in London. It is located near the ancient Tower of London but was built in the late 19th century.

Chatsworth House is one of the finest examples of a country house in England. It has been owned by the same family for 16 generations and is noted for its art collection and extensive grounds.

The Brecon Beacons National Park is located in Wales. Famous for its mountain ponies, it also boasts spectacular waterfalls and the highest mountain in southern Wales – Pen y Fan.

Famous for its 'sightings' of the mythical monster, Loch Ness is a large freshwater lake in the Highlands of Scotland.

An area of outstanding natural beauty, the Mourne Mountains contain Northern Ireland's highest peak – Slieve Donard.

? Web help

Ordnance Survey and national trails

Find out about Ordnance Survey maps:
www.ordnancesurvey.co.uk

Find out about national trails: **www.nationaltrail.co.uk**

Join the Long Distance Paths Association: **www.ldwa.org.uk**

Find out about the national parks: **www.nationalparks.gov.uk**

The National Trust

The National Trust and the National Trust for Scotland are charities which look after important buildings, gardens, coastline and countryside. You need to pay to visit the properties and gardens because they are expensive to maintain. If you like visiting National Trust buildings then you can pay a membership fee every year and visit all the places at no extra cost.

? Web help

The National Trust and the National Trust for Scotland

Find out about visiting Trust properties, joining and volunteering:

England, Wales and Northern Ireland: **www.nationaltrust.org.uk**

Scotland: **www.nts.org.uk**

! Action

Find out about National Trust properties near where you live.

Cornish pasty

British traditions

The UK's rich history has seen the development of a variety of traditions across the country. People from different regions enjoy a thriving local culture that includes specific foods, sports and leisure activities.

Traditional food

Cornish pasties are a West Country tradition. A Cornish pasty is a pastry case containing meat and vegetables. They originated as a meal for people working in the fields or mines, where their shape made them easy to carry.

Bakewell tarts come from Derbyshire. The tart has a pastry base, filled with a layer of jam and an almond filling.

Haggis comes from Scotland. It is a savoury pudding containing sheep's heart, liver and lungs, minced with onion, oatmeal, suet, spices and salt – all mixed with stock, and traditionally encased in the animal's stomach then simmered for approximately three hours.

Children dancing round a maypole

May Day has been a traditional day of festivities throughout the UK for centuries. It originates from people celebrating springtime and the fertility of the land. By 1 May, seeding the fields had been completed and the farm workers were given a day off.

Some towns and villages still hold celebrations and festivals. One traditional form of celebration is the 'Maypole' dance. This consists of pairs of boys and girls standing around the base of the pole, each holding the end of a ribbon. When the dance begins, they weave in and around each other, boys going one way and girls going the other. The ribbons are woven together around the pole until the dancers meet at the base.

Morris dancing goes back to the mid-15th century. It is performed mainly by men but there are women dancers too. There are different styles of Morris dancing across the country. Dances are performed in teams of varying numbers depending on the style. Men wear bells on their legs and clash sticks or wave handkerchiefs. You will often find them dancing outside village pubs in the summer.

Mummers plays have their origins in medieval times. They often take place in the streets. They have had a traditional place in Christmas festivities for hundreds of years and are believed to bring good luck to both performers and the people watching. The story is usually the magical re-enactment of the struggle between the powers of good and evil, or of light and darkness as autumn turns into winter and then the return of spring.

Carnivals are held in many villages and towns throughout the summer months. People dress themed vehicles, known as floats, and parade through the streets. They also compete to build the best float and prizes are awarded. Before the carnival a carnival queen and attendants are elected to lead the parade. The idea is to raise money for charity and have fun.

Cheese rolling takes place in Gloucestershire in the early summer. A large round of Double Gloucester cheese is rolled down a steep hill and people race down after it. Crowds of people come to watch. The prize for the winner is a whole cheese.

The **Olimpick Games** started in the Cotswolds in the 17th century. An actor dressed as Robert Dover, who established the first games, arrives on horseback as part of the opening ceremony. Events have included the tug of war, gymkhana, shin-kicking, motorcycle scrambling, judo, piano smashing, Morris dancing and 'dwile flonking' – a game with mops and beer! After dusk a bonfire is lit, followed by a torchlight procession to the square in Chipping Campden, where the entertainment continues well into the night.

Beating the bounds was a way of making sure people remembered the boundaries of a parish before the days of maps. The parish priest would lead the procession and check the boundary markers. Today it is more a social event and people walk, talk and enjoy a day out. It takes place in both town and country.

[!] Action

Find out about the traditional activities near where you live.

Transport

Public transport

Buses, coaches and trains criss-cross the UK.

Buses

Your local area will have bus routes designed to link villages with towns and cities. There is also a network of long-distance coaches that connect major destinations throughout the country.

Tickets

Tickets are available as single or return fare journeys. Some bus operators also offer tickets that enable you to make unlimited journeys on a given day. For example, a one-day London Travelcard allows you to travel anywhere within a series of 'zones' on the day which you bought the ticket.

Information on ticket types, routes and timetables can usually be found on your local operator's website.

Trains

The railway network carries people both long and short distances. England, Scotland and Wales are connected by fast trains between major cities. There are also local trains which carry people shorter distances. Many people use trains to commute to work in cities.

You usually need to buy a ticket before you get on a train. Sometimes, you can pay the conductor once you are on board, but this only happens if the station at which you joined the train has no staff.

Travelcards are generally available in most towns and cities. In London, you can buy an 'Oyster' card and pay for your journeys in advance. When you do this, travel is much cheaper than paying for each trip separately. Fares depend on when you travel. If it's the rush hour (when many people are travelling to or from work), fares are always more expensive. Cheaper tickets are available at less busy times, and many train operators allow you to make savings by booking early.

Some groups of people get cheaper travel. There are also discount railcards available for people over 60 years old, young people and disabled people. If you need to travel by train and bus, you may find that a PlusBus ticket offers you more flexibility.

Travelling without a ticket

If you do not have a ticket for your entire journey, you may be charged a penalty fine. This would probably cost you more than the price of the ticket. Make sure you buy the most appropriate ticket for your journey and don't be afraid to ask the ticket office or the station staff for help before you board your train.

? Web help

Public transport

For railways: www.nationalrail.co.uk

For railways in Northern Ireland: www.translink.co.uk

For local buses and trains anywhere: www.traveline.info

For coaches: www.nationalexpress.com

For coaches in Scotland: www.citylink.co.uk

For coaches in Northern Ireland: www.translink.co.uk

PlusBus: www.plusbus.info

Taxis

Taxis are available to hire for people who can't or don't want to use public transport. They are often expensive but may be essential if no public transport is available or if it is difficult to use. For example, some people with disabilities or lots of luggage can find public transport difficult. Sometimes the time of day can also make the use of a taxi more convenient.

Official taxis have meters which calculate the charge you will have to pay. It can vary according to the distance, the time of day and the time the journey takes. They can be hailed on the street. London taxis have an orange light on the front to show they are available for hire.

Minicabs are also licensed for hire. They must be booked before the journey as they are not allowed to pick up passengers on the street.

All taxis and minicabs must be licensed and display a licence plate to operate legally. If they do not have a licence, they are not insured for fare-paying passengers and cannot be guaranteed to be safe. You should not use unlicensed minicabs as you do not know the intentions of the driver.

Driving

Licences and tests

In the UK, we drive on the left. As a UK resident, you are allowed to drive for 12 months if you have a driving licence from another country, but most people will then need to take a UK driving test. If you come from an EU country, you can drive until your licence runs out. There is a group of countries which have special arrangements with the UK so that you can exchange your licence for the equivalent British licence. These are: Australia, Barbados, British Virgin Islands, Canada, Falkland Islands, Hong Kong, Japan, Monaco, New Zealand, Singapore, South Africa, Switzerland and Zimbabwe.

Holders of ordinary licences from the Faroe Islands and South Korea can also do the same.

You must be 17 years or older to drive a car or motorcycle, 18 to drive a medium-sized lorry and 21 to drive a large lorry or bus.

Web help

Do I need a licence?

www.gov.uk/driving-nongb-licence

While you are learning to drive you must have a provisional licence. You also need to have someone over the age of 21, who has had a full licence for at least three years, sitting beside you. Your car must have 'L' plates on the front and back to warn other drivers that you are inexperienced.

Web help

Your provisional driving licence

www.gov.uk/apply-first-provisional-driving-licence

The driving test is made up of a theory test and a practical test. The theory test is taken online, at centres across the country. You must pass this before you go on to take the practical test. The same applies if you ride a motorbike. There are two parts to the test. The first part is a multiple choice test, where you answer questions with several possible answers on a computer screen. The second is a hazard perception test, where you have to respond to hazards shown in a series of video clips. You take both parts of the test on the same day at the same test centre. To move on to the practical test, you must pass both parts.

The practical test asks you to show that you can drive on different types of road and in different conditions. It also wants you to show that you know the Highway Code (which states how you should behave on the road), and can apply it.

When you arrive for your practical test you will need both parts of your driving licence (photocard and paper licence) and your theory test certificate. If you do not have these with you, your test will be cancelled and you will lose the fee that you have paid.

Before the practical exam, the examiner will test your eyesight and ask you two practical questions about the car. The test involves both following the examiner's instructions and showing that you can drive safely while making decisions for yourself.

After the test, the examiner will tell you whether you've passed or explain why you haven't. If you have passed, you can start driving straight away. Your full licence will be sent to you in the post. If you fail, you must wait at least ten days before you can take the test again.

In Northern Ireland, you must display an 'R' plate – meaning restricted – for a year after your test.

Once you have your licence, you can drive until you are aged 70. When you reach that age, you will need to renew it. Thereafter you will need to renew your licence every three years.

There are many driving schools that will help you with both the theory and practical tests.

? **Web help**

Taking the driving tests

Find out about the theory test: www.gov.uk/driving-theory-test

Practise the theory test:
www.gov.uk/practise-your-driving-theory-test

Book your theory test: www.gov.uk/book-a-driving-theory-test

The Highway Code: www.gov.uk/highway-code

Find out about the practical driving test:
www.gov.uk/practical-driving-test-for-cars

Book your practical driving test:
www.gov.uk/book-practical-driving-test

For a range of informative driving materials designed to help you pass your test:
www.tsoshop.co.uk/bookstore.asp

! **Action**

Do you want to drive in the UK?

Do you need driving lessons? Find out about driving schools near you.

You and your car

What you must do

If you bring your car to the UK, you can drive it with foreign plates for six months in a 12-month period. It must be registered and taxed in the country where it came from.

After this six-month period, it must be taxed with the Driver and Vehicle Licensing Agency (DVLA) in the UK.

 Web help

Registering your car

www.gov.uk/vehicle-registration/overview

You must tax your car. The amount you will pay depends on the size of the car and its environmental efficiency. If you have a car that is not going to be driven on public roads then you do not need to pay – but you do need to inform DVLA and get a document to prove that this is the case. You can tax your car online or at the post office.

If your car is not taxed, it may be clamped or towed away and you will have to pay a fine.

 Web help

Taxing your car

www.gov.uk/calculate-vehicle-tax-rates

www.gov.uk/tax-disc

Insuring your car is compulsory. You must have third-party insurance but most people have comprehensive insurance. There are many companies offering car insurance. You must be careful to tell the truth when you apply for it because it will be void if you don't, which means you will not be insured.

It you drive without insurance, expect a heavy fine and up to six penalty points on your licence. This will make your insurance more expensive in future. It is also an offence to let someone drive your car if they haven't got insurance.

 Web help

Insuring your car

www.gov.uk/vehicle-insurance/overview

If your car is three years old or more, it must be tested for safety every 12 months. This is known as an MOT test and can be carried out at any approved garage. If the car passes you will be given a certificate. It is illegal to drive a car over three years old without an up-to-date MOT certificate. Without an MOT, your insurance will be invalid. You will also need the certificate when you tax your car.

[**?**] **Web help**

The MOT test

Find out more about the MOT:
www.gov.uk/getting-an-mot/the-mot-test

Driving your car

The UK's road network is made up of four main classifications of roads: motorways, dual carriageways, and single-carriageway 'A' and 'B' roads.

Motorways and dual carriageways are designed for high-speed travel. They connect major centres of population with one another and have two or more lanes running in each direction.

'A' roads also provide routes to major destinations. They sometimes have two lanes (dual carriageways) in each direction and are usually well signposted from other routes. In places such as the Scottish Highlands there are fewer roads and a narrow, single-track road may be classified as an 'A' road because it is the only route available.

'B' roads connect villages and rural locations. They are usually narrower, less direct routes.

Narrow roads in rural areas are not classified and there may not be signposts at every turning to help you find your way. If you meet a vehicle coming from the other direction, one of you may need to reverse to the nearest 'passing place'.

Wearing seat belts is compulsory for all passengers. Children under 12 who are below 135 cm in height must use a child seat or booster seat.

Keeping to the speed limit is compulsory. The speed limits are:

- 30 miles per hour (mph) in towns and other built-up areas, unless a sign shows a different limit.
- 60 mph on single carriageways.
- 70 mph on motorways and dual carriageways.

The speed limits may be lower if you are towing a trailer or driving different sorts of vehicles.

Driving when over the alcohol limit is illegal. If you have more than 35 microgrammes per 100 millilitres of breath or a blood alcohol level of more than 80 milligrammes per 100 millilitres of blood you must not drive.

If the police think you are driving unsafely, they can stop you and give you a test to see how much alcohol you have in your body. This is known as a breathalyser test. If you are 'over the limit' and have more than the permitted amount of alcohol or refuse to take the test, you will be arrested.

If you drink and drive you can expect to pay a large fine and be disqualified from driving for a long period. You will have to do a retraining course and take your driving test again before getting your licence back.

Take care if you are taking medicine, because this can affect your ability to drive. You should check with your GP or pharmacist. The packaging will often have information about side effects too.

Stopping after an accident is compulsory. If you are involved in an accident, it is an offence not to stop. If the accident is not serious and no one is hurt, you just need to exchange details with the other driver. If people are hurt, dial 999 and call an ambulance. The police will also arrive and decide whether there has been a criminal offence.

Leisure

Activities in your local community

Most communities have a variety of organisations you might join – depending on your interests. (For example, there may be clubs for people who like gardening, sewing or cycling.) Some organisations are national, with local branches, others are purely local. They are all usually run by enthusiasts in your community. Joining such organisations is an excellent way of getting to know people where you live.

There are so many different sorts of groups that it is impossible to list them here. Your local paper, the internet and notices in shops and public offices can help you find out what's going on. Many local council websites have lists of organisations and events that are taking place.

Here is a selection of organisations which have a national network of branches:

- **Oxfam**: you can get involved to support its work in developing countries.
- **Greenpeace**: if you are interested in the environment, the organisation will welcome your support.
- **Royal Society for the Protection of Birds**: has local groups you can join.
- **The Ramblers**: if you are interested in walks through the countryside.
- **Embroiderers' Guild**: for people who like stitching.
- **Women's Institute**: holds weekly meetings with speakers on a wide range of issues.
- **National Childbirth Trust**: supports parents and offers classes for those expecting a baby.
- **National Women's Register**: for talks and discussions.
- **University of the Third Age**: offers courses for older people.

? Web help

National organisations

If you have online access, just search the name of an organisation or your particular interest and you'll be sure to find a useful link.

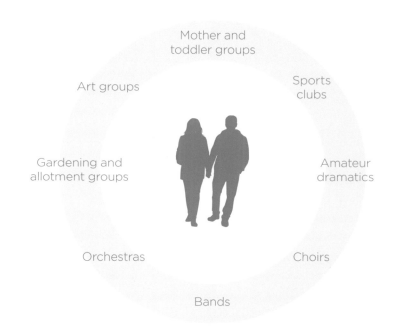

Mother and
toddler groups

Art groups

Sports
clubs

Gardening and
allotment groups

Amateur
dramatics

Orchestras

Choirs

Bands

Some of the activities you may find in your local area

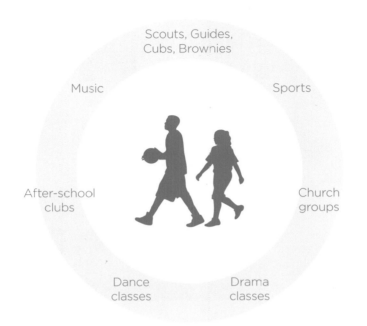

Scouts, Guides, Cubs, Brownies

Music

Sports

After-school clubs

Church groups

Dance classes

Drama classes

Some of the activities you may find in your local area that are specifically aimed at children

 Action

Look at your local council website and see the range of activities that are available in your local area.

Leisure at home

Television and radio

TV and radio are popular ways of passing time. There are many different TV channels. Some of them are free to view and others are only available on subscription. Soap operas such as *EastEnders* and *Coronation Street* are watched by millions of people. Talent shows such as *Strictly Come Dancing* and *The X Factor* are also very popular. You will find many programmes about current affairs, the natural environment and new drama. There are also programmes in Welsh and Gaelic.

If you watch live TV on a television set, computer, tablet or any other device, you must have a TV licence. Once you have a licence, all the equipment in your home is covered. If, however, you live in a shared house where everyone has a separate tenancy agreement, you will all need a separate licence.

A TV licence is free for people over the age of 75, and blind people get a 50% discount.

If you watch live TV but do not buy a licence, you will have to pay a fine of up to £1000.

 **Web help**

TV licensing

Find out how to buy a licence and how much it will cost:

www.tvlicensing.co.uk

The money from your TV licence supports the British Broadcasting Corporation – or the BBC as it is widely known. It is a public service broadcaster providing television and radio programmes to the UK and the world. It is state funded but independent of government. Other channels are funded through advertisements. The BBC is the world's largest broadcaster.

There are many different radio stations in the UK. Some are national – others are local. If you want to find out about what's happening where you live, local radio is a good source of information.

Some radio stations specialise in certain types of music and others broadcast in regional languages such as Welsh or Gaelic. Many are funded by advertising. BBC radio stations are funded from the TV licence. There are a number of national BBC radio stations which are a med at specific audiences. There are specialist music and regional stations and the Asian network which is aimed at people from the Indian sub-continent.

- Radio 1 plays pop music
- Radio 2 plays easy listening music
- Radio 3 plays classical music
- Radio 4 specialises in the spoken word and is responsible for a range of output including politics, currents affairs, original drama and comedy
- Radio 5 Live focuses on news and sport.

Other leisure pursuits

Cooking and entertaining is enjoyed by many people in the UK. People invite friends for a meal in their homes. Cooking often involves meals which originate in the UK and from a wide range of other countries. There are many programmes on TV and books which show people how to cook interesting food to share with their friends.

Gardening is popular because many people have gardens, which they want to look good. In some cases, people grow fruit and vegetables to eat at home. Even people who live in flats have window boxes, where they grow flowers and herbs. There are produce shows across the country where people win prizes for the best flowers, fruit and vegetables. You can rent an allotment if you want to grow more produce. The local council will be able to help. In some areas they are very popular and there are long waiting lists.

Pets are kept by many people. Cats and dogs are popular, as well as small mammals such as hamsters and guinea pigs. There are laws about keeping a range of more exotic animals.

If you take your dog for a walk in a public place, it must wear a collar showing the name and address of the owner. You are responsible for keeping your dog under control and for cleaning up after it in a public place. You can be fined if you do not do this.

It is against the law to treat a pet cruelly or to neglect it. Pets should be vaccinated to protect them from a range of diseases.

Social networking is used by many people to stay in touch with friends at home and abroad. Facebook allows people to share photos, videos and general discussion. Some people use social media to organise social events and arrange charity fund raisers. You can use your phone to keep up to date with what's going on. Twitter gives people the opportunity to exchange ideas about current events and keep up to date with people they are interested in. Skype is very useful because you can talk to people face to face anywhere in the world, if your contacts also have an internet connection. It has the great advantage of being free.

Going out

Shopping

The local high street offers many opportunities for shopping. Town centres have a range of chain stores and some independent shops which sell more individual products.

Shopping malls are usually under cover and can be found in town centres. They house many different shops, including fashion stores, department stores and electrical retailers. People also take trips to retail parks on the outskirts of towns and cities.

Most chain stores in the UK are open seven days a week and small shops can open every day for as long as they like. In England and Wales, most large shops can only open for six hours on a Sunday.

Cinema

Going to the movies is a popular outing Cinemas show films for children and adults There is a classification system to help you work out whether a film is suitable for a particular age group. It is also used for DVDs.

- **U**: Universal – anyone can see it.
- **PG**: Parental Guidance films have no age limit but parents should be aware that there might be some violence or other activity that might upset a child below the age of 8.
- **12A/12**: A 12A film means that a child under the age of 12 is only allowed to see the film in a cinema if they have an adult with them. The same film on DVD is classified as 12, meaning that anyone over the age of 12 can rent or buy it.
- **15**: Age 15 and over.
- **18**: Adults only – can contain violence, sex or verbal abuse.

Pubs and clubs

Pubs and nightclubs are places where people may go to meet their friends. You must be aged 18 or over to drink alcohol on licensed premises. It is against the law for younger people to drink alcohol or for adults to buy alcohol for younger people. However, if you're 16 or 17 and accompanied by an adult, you are allowed to drink (but not buy) beer, wine or cider with a meal in a restaurant.

The person who runs the pub or nightclub can decide on its opening hours. Many pubs close after lunch and open again in the evening. In busy places, they may stay open all day. They often close at 11 pm but may stay open later.

Betting and gambling

Betting and gambling often takes place at sporting events. You can also go to a betting shop or casino to gamble if you are older than 18. The National Lottery is drawn every Saturday and Wednesday. If you're older than 16, you can buy a ticket for the draw or a scratch card for an immediate result. The money people spend on tickets goes to help good causes as well as being given away as prizes.

 Action

What's your interest?

What sort of leisure activities do you enjoy? Find out about social venues near where you live.

Glossary

Anglican Church	The officially established Church of England
cabinet	A senior group of government ministers who are responsible for making decisions
conveyancer	A legal expert trained in the aspects of the law that deal with property
corporation tax	A tax on the profits of limited companies
denomination	A sub-group of an established religious tradition
dialect	A regional variation of a language (for example, the Yorkshire dialect of English)
estate	The money, property, debts and possessions left behind after death
estate agent	A person or business that arranges the selling, renting or management of properties
Human Rights Act	An Act of Parliament designed to ensure that public organisations treat everyone equally
National Health Service (NHS)	The health service provided by the state

National Insurance	A series of payments deducted from the salaries of people below state pension age. The money is used to fund the health service and the benefits system.
Ofsted	The official body that regulates schools and other services for children
Parliament	The seat of the UK government
pension	A system of payments made to people after they retire
Prime Minister	The leader of the government
registrar	An official responsible for recording births, deaths and marriages
solicitor	A lawyer qualified to give legal advice to clients. They may also represent clients in some courts and instruct other legal professionals working on their clients' behalf.
value added tax (VAT)	A tax applied to some goods and services

Index